A WAY TO WHITHORN

A Way to Whithorn

A Guide to the
Whithorn Pilgrim Way
through the Machars of Galloway

Andrew Patterson

SAINT ANDREW PRESS
EDINBURGH

*The Publisher acknowledges
financial assistance from
The Drummond Trust towards the
publication of this volume.*

First published in 1993 by
SAINT ANDREW PRESS
121 George Street, Edinburgh EH2 4YN

ISBN 0 7152 0690 7

British Library Cataloguing in Publication Data
A catalogue record for this book
is available from the British Library

ISBN 0715206907

Book design and cover concept by Mark Blackadder.
Cover photographs (background and inserts)
by Paul Turner.
Cover photographs (ariel) by Colin Hopper.
Cover Celtic batik by Ros Plant.
Photograph of batik by Walter Bell.
Text illustrations on pp 10, 25, 30, 35, 56, 64, 80, 81,
96, 106, 116, 142, 148, 149, 154 by Steve Dowling .
Text illustrations on pp 23, 26, 45, 67 by Dave Pollock.
Text photographs on pp 4, 7, 34, 43, 53, 57, 157, 160,
162 by Paul Turner.
Text photographs (ariel) on pp 34, 137, 150 by Colin
Hopper.

Typeset in 11.5/15 pt Garamond.
Printed and **bound** by Athenaeum Press Ltd, Newcastle
upon Tyne.

CONTENTS

FOREWORD

by Martin Palmer

WORLD WIDE FUND FOR NATURE

I FIRST came to Whithorn drawn by the prayers, poems and insights of the great Celtic saints and the model of their monasticism, derived from the example of St Ninian. In their writings, these great men and women of God spoke of the everyday and ordinary as being extraordinary through the infusion of the love of the Trinity. It was this vision which drew me north and in particular to walk the old routes associated with Ninian. How I wish I'd had Andrew's book with me then! For here, in twentieth century language, is that same ability to look at the ordinary and everyday and suffuse them with the power of the Trinity and the insights of the saints.

This book is no sentimental journey or romantic trip back into a long gone past. It is a modern pilgrimage amongst the beauties of nature, the battery farms of agro-business, the tawdriness of modern buildings and the rush of the great roads— an encounter with Galloway past, present and to some extent future, through the medium of an ancient walk. We are asked to look below the surface, hear the stories, see the anomalies and catch a glimpse now

and then of different pictures of the Kingdom of God on earth.

Weaving legend, history, observation,
environmental concern, economic and social
reality and geography together into a seam-
less whole, the author invites us to step out
into a landscape which tells us about the
perennial struggle of human beings to make
sense of their world, the desire to celebrate
life and to respond to that of God in every-
one and everything. For those who think
that such a walk is an escape from the real
world, Andrew shows that real world laid
bare and yet with hope at its centre.

When I first visited St Ninian's cave, I
too walked the old pilgrims' route down
the little stream to the seashore. As I came
closer to the shoreline, I heard a strange
flapping sound, like the wraps of a shroud.
I could not identify what this was until I
rounded the corner and saw that every bush
and shrub at the mouth of the little river
that runs into the sea, was covered in plastic
blown in from the sea. I stood shocked and
was forced to ask myself what relevance did
Celtic spirituality have to this harsh reality.

This book provides many of the answers.
It asks us, in its own quiet way, to reflect on
what we see and to undertake not just a
journey over a given geographical area, but
perhaps a journey inwards, to see ourselves
and the world we are making, in a new light
—the light of Christ and of his creation.

There was a path that once I knew,
wound with bright ivies and trumpeting
haws, of whitest sand embroidered with
flowers,
that very few had taken.
~ INCREDIBLE STRING BAND ~

A CROSS AT NINIAN'S CAVE

Autumn, rudderless and low
tracked by dark eyed jurors
their tight knuckles blank as snow
I rest between red palms of rock
marvel at membrane, musk, and pulse of sea;
leave, behind a veil of twinkling amulets
a votive for Ninian, Mother Earth,
and the Silence in me.
~ TOM POW ~

THE ROLE OF HISTORY IS NOT
TO APPORTION BLAME IN THE
PAST BUT TO DISCERN A
BETTER WAY
INTO THE FUTURE.
~ KARL MARX ~

PROLOGUE
by Andrew Patterson

THIS book has been written as an introduction to one of the least frequented
parts of Scotland. Walking and cycling are
the best ways of getting to know the landscape and Galloway has many rewards for
her visitors.

Often city people lead their lives among
the noise and pollution of heavy traffic. It
can be a deeply healing experience to escape
into the greenery, to hear the soft breath of
cattle, or see the flitting of a wren through
shadows. However, traffic these days invades
the countryside too, and walking on narrow
and winding roads can be alarming as forty
ton lorries hurtle past the ear drums. So
please be careful.

Scottish tradition enables ramblers to
wander freely in the uplands where fencing
is sparse, but the intensive agriculture of
the lowlands has spread barbed wire in a
dense mesh of barriers, some of which are
electrified. Whilst many farmers greet the
rambler with friendly courtesy, others can
be suspicious and dour. So, walking cross
country in lowland Scotland is not an easy
option, especially when many ancient rights
of way have fallen into disuse and neglect.

But, take heart—this book offers a guide to a route which avoids busy roads as much as it does the farmer's barbed wire. It takes the reader on a journey, on two feet or two wheels, to discover the loveliness of one special part of the Lowlands of Scotland. To aid this journey, the Whithorn Pilgrimage Trust and Dumfries and Galloway Regional Council, with help also from Scottish Natural Heritage and Galloway Groundbase, have recently signposted a walking and cycling route from Glenluce to Whithorn, through the long peninsula of the Machars of Galloway.

The soil of the Machars was where the earliest Christian community in northern Europe put down deep roots and began to flourish. In later centuries Whithorn became the major focus of pilgrimage, rivalling Iona and St Andrews for the attention of kings.

Iona has its beautiful white beaches and the astonishing loveliness of the Hebrides. St Andrews has the clarity and brightness of an east coast jewel with the Grampians as a dramatic background—but the Machars have their own delights. Whithorn has been called 'Whithorn of the Five Kingdoms' because of the beauty of its situation. Standing with feet in Scotland the eyes can travel overseas to the distant hills of Ulster, the Isle of Man, and to England as well. What exactly is meant by 'the fifth kingdom'?

Well, as a local saying tells us, 'look above, heaven is all around.'

Walking through the Machars there are echoes of Eden to soothe the refugee from commuter snarl-up and computer screen. Indeed the purpose of the Whithorn Pilgrimage Trust is to encourage walkers and cyclists to discover the quiet miles of the Whithorn Pilgrim Way. It is a new addition to the growing lattice of long distance footpaths like the Pennine and Southern Uplands Ways with which it connects. Its miles on moor and coast are as lovely as any.

Near the village of Glenluce the Pilgrim Way enters the parish of Kirkcowan. A local saying declares 'out of the world and into Kirkcowan.' Believe me, it's true!

~ *Kirkinner 1993* ~

*This book is dedicated to
the work of the*
WORLD WIDE FUND
FOR NATURE
*so that love and respect
for the countryside can be increased.*

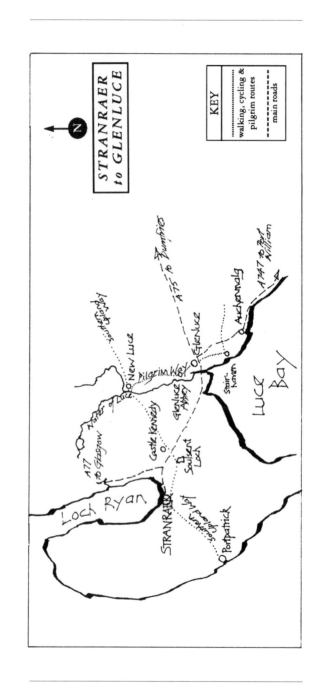

1

STRANRAER *to* GLENLUCE

GALLOWAY is still a green and lovely land which smiles with flowers in their seasons. Its remoteness from industrial cities has saved it from despoliation, and its population is scattered thinly in small towns and villages. Hunched against the Atlantic winds and distanced from the rest of Scotland by long moors and huge forestry plantations, fingers of land stretch south in a coastline of bays and peninsulas.

The lines of Tom Pow's poem 'In Old Galloway' (*The Moth Trap*, Canongate Press, Edinburgh, 1990) describe the intangible qualities of the landscape:

> *Turf was torn from rich earth*
> *and laid on poor; a wealth*
> *of dykes conjured up*
> *the steepest slopes—till a green*
> *democracy was everywhere.*
>
> *On bright summer evenings,*
> *grasslands lit from within,*
> *where would a child not go?*
> *Up the hawthorns, over the hill*
> *to Away! Of course it's a lie:*
> *this land too is rucked*

with the bones and blood
guide books never chart.
In early spring, we pluck
little white knuckles from rich
dark moss—the kind that lines
the most comfortable
contours of our hearts.

This green democracy waits to welcome its visitors. The main port of Galloway is Stranraer where ships from Ireland connect with frequent buses and trains from Glasgow and London. This busy little town lies some ten miles to the west of the point where the Pilgrim Way begins in lonely moorland beside the swiftly flowing Water of Luce.

Stiff after hours in ferry, bus or train, many a walker will be keen to begin the journey to Whithorn in Stranraer itself, although a local bus service links the town with the quiet village of Glenluce which is situated on the route of the Pilgrim Way. If you decide against the bus, the walk begins in the harbour area where, mixing with the softer Scottish accents of Galloway, are the rich vowels of Ireland.

Skirting the edge of town is the Southern Upland Way which goes east all the way to the North Sea. The pavements of Stranraer's small suburbia are soon replaced by the tranquil lochs at the evocatively named Soulseat Abbey, little of which remains amid the quiet pastures.

At the village of Castle Kennedy the long distance footpath enters the extensive gardens of the Earl of Stair. Eucalyptus, sequoia and sweet chestnut scent the air already heavy with thousands of flowers in season.

Beyond the gardens the route rises up over Glenwhan moor and its more recent plantations of single crop spruce until the wooded valley at New Luce village where the first of the Whithorn Pilgrim Way signposts point to the south. Note that they do not bear the thistle emblem of the Southern Upland Way, but carry the distinctive circle-cross, a design associated with the early Celtic Church of Whithorn, founded, tradition insists, by a bishop called Ninian in AD 398.

The tarmac road from New Luce southwards to Glenluce village is not suitable for walkers, being narrow and winding. The Pilgrim Way, however, keeps to tracks which follow the ridge of hills to the east of the Water of Luce. Above Cruise Farm the path passes by an Iron Age fort. Huge mounds of rubble are the remnants of an immense, stone rampart which once crowned the hill. Mortar was not used, the dry-stone construction being strengthened instead by an interlace of timber that has long since rotted away.

From this vantage point the walls of Glenluce Abbey can be seen, the soaring

arches ending sadly in roofless ruin. It was
founded by Cistercian monks eight hundred
years ago when Rolland was Lord of
Galloway. The men who established the
Abbey came from France and settled here
under Rolland's protection. Today it is a
quiet place in the care of Historic Scotland.

Cistercians usually chose remote, sparsely
populated places in the wilderness to build
their austere architecture. They were fine
builders and used local stone, slate and
timber. Among their number were water
engineers who constructed fish ponds,
sluices and mills among the fields. Capable
farmers gathered great harvests of grain and
wool, much of which was exported to the
continent in sailing ships constructed out
of sawn timber.

The Cistercians were men of considerable enterprise and their labour made them
wealthy and powerful throughout the
district. However, much of the work and

GLENLUCE ABBEY

some of the profit of this religious community went into caring for the many travellers
who rested with them before setting out on
the final miles for Whithorn.

One building in the Abbey is still
spanned by its vaulted, mediaeval roof: the
chapter house, where learned discussion
weighed the events of the day, the Abbot's
decisions being enforced by vows of obed-
ience. Cistercian monks were often wise,
literate men and would have discussed
issues other than leather, wool and grain, or
the rents and obligations owed by the native
peasantry in the surrounding hills.

The Cistercians enjoyed nearly four
centuries in their secluded valley, under the
protection of the Lords of Galloway and the
Kings of Scots, until 1560 when the
Scottish Reformation ended their control in
Glenluce. It was their wealth and power
which eventually brought them envy and
unpopularity. The office of Abbot had
degenerated into a position of worldly
status to be bought and sold by the younger
sons of the nobility.

But the early years of the Reformation
were not harsh in Scotland. The remaining
monks received a pension and were allowed
to grow old in peace, while, throughout
Scotland, the extensive estates of the old
Roman Catholic Church were appropriated
by the gentry.

Revenues of the Roman Church in

Scotland were ten times that enjoyed by the
King of Scots, and much of this wealth was
sent to Italy year after year. This 'balance of
payments' crisis was as much a cause for
the Reformation as theological innovation.
Scotland felt it could no longer afford to
support financially the Roman pontiff in the
manner to which he had become accustomed.

In return for the taking over of ecclesiastical lands, the gentry undertook to provide
for the new Protestant parishes, but without
an income to maintain them, the great
cathedral and abbey churches in Scotland
fell into disrepair. Here, at Glenluce, the
venerable Cistercian buildings were reduced
to a handy source of building material for
the domestic requirements of the neighbourhood. Indeed, it was the last Abbot himself
who stripped the lead from the roof, and
then the timber, tumbling the walls of
cloister, nave, hospice and dormitory to
build himself a strong tower at Castle of
Park a mile down river. Thus, many of the
walls of the substantial farmhouses in the
valley will have been built with stone from
the Abbey.

Rest and seclusion are still to be found
in this place, but the beauty of the monks'
haunting plainsong is only a lingering
memory. However, there is a certain music
in the lowing of cattle and the sound of the
flowing river.

The path from the Abbey to Glenluce

village rises up over the well named Fineview Hill. It follows the ancient pilgrim
road, avoiding the tarmac in the valley
below. The horizon looms wide up on the
hill, and moorland and conifer plantations
stretch north, east and west. Before turning
south to the ten mile sweep of sand dunes
and marram grass which heads Luce Bay,
why not pause for a moment on Fineview
and look over Gleniron Fell swelling to the
north? Huge mounds constructed out of
hundreds of tons of stones stand witness to
the lives of the people of Galloway who lived
four thousand years ago, before Abraham
left Iraq for the Jordan. These mounds, or
tumuli, contained chambers used for com-
munal burials for ancient generations. This
tribal burial ground is no less a statement
of reverence before the mystery of life and
death than the relatively young walls of the
Christian Abbey.

The dead bones of these early Galloway

GLENIRON BURIAL MOUND

people tell few tales, but we know that they lived scattered across the landscape in simple, round houses, learning to become farmers. At first, hand-tilled gardens co-existed with pastoral skills as half wild sheep, cattle and pigs were domesticated in similar ways to those of the modern Laplanders with reindeer. Soon the small gardens became square fields tilled by ox-drawn ploughs. Then they began to smelt copper, lead, silver and gold, but, despite the name, the people of Gleniron did not know about the grey, hard iron which belonged to later, more warlike times when the fort was built at Cruise Farm.

The Bronze Age people left their mark on Galloway and the Pilgrim Way passes many of their other memorials. They lived in an international culture when skin boats with woven sails, much like the traditional Irish *curragh*, would skim along the coastlines of Atlantic Europe in the short months of summer. Their temples were the standing stones and circles raised from Portugal to Denmark in the millennia following 5000 BC until after 1500 BC. Their more than four thousand years of gradually developing continuity knew a stability little known in the nearly four thousand years which followed.

Fineview Hill deserves its name—all Wigtownshire spreads out before it. It is the underlying rock which forms the contours of the landscape. Laid down in shallow seas during the Ordovician era of geological development, in a timescale that dwarfs the thousands of years of evolving human history, these bedrocks were slowly formed and moulded. For two hundred million years the sedimentary muds and shales from the Ordovician sea floor were twisted and changed by the impacts and rendings of the European and American continents as they have slowly eased across the surface of the spinning globe. These imperceptible movements tore the planet's crust allowing massive intrusions of molten, igneous rock to well up and form the great hills of inland Galloway.

Ice Ages ground the bedrock, smoothing contours and smearing great drumlin mounds of clay upon its surface. Glaciers, thousands of feet thick, moulded the shape of valley and moor, a shape only revealed by a thaw so complete that the ocean swept in to sever Ireland from Britain, and both from Europe. Then a dank and naked tundra advanced in the wake of the ice until it too warmed, and oak, ash, pine, birch and juniper grew into a dense tangle and everything teemed with life.

The hundred or so centuries of human life in Galloway began when summer camps of hunters and fishermen stained the sky with the smoke of their cooking fires. These human centuries have altered the soft south-west of Scotland as radically as crunching continents or sequences of Ice Ages. These days, the pace of feet or pedal can reveal much of that story because the bones of the landscape carry the imprint of each successive generation, and none more so than the machine-orientated upheavals of recent years.

The glittering horizon of Luce Bay beckons. Beyond woodlands and the wild headlands the Pilgrim Way weaves to its destination—and the wilderness can be felt, banging in the blood of life.

GLENLUCE *to* MOCHRUM

GLENLUCE village is like many other undemonstrative little towns in southern Scotland, built out of local stone, with a collection of more recent housing clustering round the old main street. It was, until recently, a much busier place with heavy traffic rushing to and from the Irish ferries. A bypass has now restored tranquillity to the village. Being in a rush is not really in the nature of Glenluce even though the exports and imports of half of Ireland stream through the fields around it in massive lorries on the new Euroroute of the A75.

The Pilgrim Way enters the village over a disused railway cutting, and wends past the parish kirk. The kirk's undulating roof supports heavy, modern tiles on elderly timbers, and has old, stone walls covered in harling. The grip which the Presbyterian Church of Scotland once held over the life of the nation is far less than it used to be. Until just after World War II, hundreds of people regularly worshipped in this old kirk. It became the hub of community life in the centuries after Glenluce Abbey was deserted, organising care for the sick, elderly

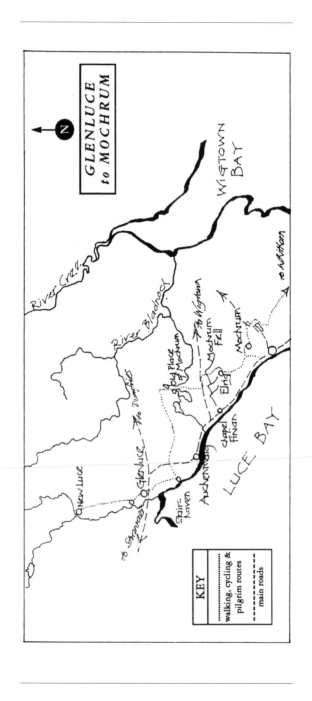

GLENLUCE to MOCHRUM

N

River Cree

WIGTOWN BAY

River Bladnoch

to Wigtown

Old Place of Mochrum

Mochrum Fell

Elrig

Mochrum

to Whithorn

New Luce

Glenluce — The Dumfries

Chapel Finian

Airlywhang

LUCE BAY

to Stranraer

Stair-haven

KEY

- - - walking, cycling &
pilgrim routes

– – – main roads

and fatherless. Like the other parishes throughout Scotland, it organised an education system that produced one of the first literate peasantries in the world—a great achievement. Although its role has diminished in the modern world, this simple, grey building is still the continuing focus of many lives in the neighbourhood.

Today the indifference of the majority to matters of religion is a problem the modern church community has to contend with, but earlier Presbyterians had to struggle for their egalitarian freedoms against more hierarchical and feudal notions of the nature of social order. They were often in conflict with the Stuart kings, by that time based in London—a Scottish dynasty ruling a United Kingdom. For most of the seventeenth century the monarchy tried to impose bishops on the Scottish Church so that it would conform with the Episcopalian Church of England. They also viewed the free debate of the Presbyterian General Assembly in Edinburgh with alarm as it was thought to constitute a threat to the civil power of the crown.

The stubborn and subversive Presbyterians defied the kings down south until open warfare prevailed. English monarchs had claimed to be head of the Church of England since the time of Henry VIII, but no King of Scots had ever made that same claim to dominance over the Scottish

Church. Many Scots were outraged. Those
who ignored the claims of the Stuart kings
in London insisted that the only head of any
Church was the carpenter from Nazareth—
'Christ the King!' was the rallying cry of
the Scottish resistance.

Circumstances boiled over when a huge
petition was signed in favour of national
autonomy in Church organisation. This
National Covenant was a direct challenge
to King Charles I, a single-minded man who
believed in the divine right of the king to
rule without encumbrance.

But his attitude brought problems to
his southern kingdom as well. The English
Parliament quarrelled with the royal
autocrat. Reduced to rule by decree and
deprived of revenue by Parliament, Charles
was unable to stop the invasion of northern
England by a Scottish army.

This expedition was not in the manner
of the cruel warfare of previous centuries
between the old antagonists, when thatch
was indiscriminately fired, wells poisoned
with the corpses of children, crops ruined,
and livestock driven off leaving the sur-
vivors to face famine. This time the army of
the Scottish Covenanters was tightly
disciplined. It paid for its provisions with
Baltic silver, and its ranks were filled with
veterans who had fought with the Protestant
armies of northern Germany against the
Roman Catholic south. Their general, a

man called Alexander Leslie (1580-1661), was a master of mobile warfare, and the conduct of his troops did not alienate the north country English. On the contrary, their psalm singing reassured a troubled population that there would be no murder or mayhem.

Newcastle was captured, and with its fall London lost its fuel supply as the new year of 1640 began. London, already a city of several hundred thousand people strung out along the tidal River Thames, depended upon this vital trade in coal from the estuaries of the Tyne and Wear. It was a bitterly cold winter in the capital and the king's popularity plummeted with the temperatures. The English Parliament was emboldened to challenge King Charles and the English Civil War began. As a result, the embryo of parliamentary democracy was established, and with it the rights of the ordinary people in a society still dominated by the aristocracy.

In the early years of the war the Scottish Army of the Covenant stiffened the untried levies of the English Parliamentarians against Royalist Cavaliers, until the development of Oliver Cromwell's regiments of Ironsides which shattered Royalist hopes of victory over the rebels.

However, when Charles II returned to the throne after the death of Cromwell in 1659, a terrible time of persecution began for those Presbyterians who openly supported the Covenant, resisting the imposition of the king's bishops on the Scottish Church. Garrisons of royalist dragoons were billeted in those areas of Scotland which showed resistance. Most of the country sullenly acquiesced, but Galloway remained stubborn. Only when the last Stuart king, James VII and II, was evicted from Britain in 1688 did the 'killing times' of religious persecution end in Galloway.

Throughout Wigtownshire, the Stewartry of Kirkcudbright, and Dumfriesshire are the graves of hundreds of martyrs who were killed where they were caught by the king's dragoons. Worse befell those who were captured alive. Torture, public execution, or transportation to the sugar plantations of the Caribbean were the fate of hundreds more, dying in defence of the freedom of conscience.

The hammering of the 'killing times' produced a hard, strong, puritanical form of Christianity. Its ideas and idealism undeniably helped the emergence of democracy, not least in the influence it had on the phrasing eventually of the American Constitution. But to many closer to home it had become the enemy of colour and warmth, frowning on mirth and music, smothering dance, theatre and all the arts which make life delightful, with its severe disapproval. The Kirk came to be seen as an alien killjoy by large sections of the national community who resented the threats of hellfire and a God who was presented to them more as an awful judge than a loving parent.

Following this alienation, modern science has at times seemed to declare the redundancy of the notion of there being a God who created the universe with a purpose that put human life on earth at the centre of a divine, unfolding plan. Charles Darwin's theory of evolution overturned the traditional view of the literal (as opposed to metaphysical) truth of scripture, until Bertrand Russell could declare that a human being is no more than 'an accident-ally met collection of atoms'. There is no room for divine compassion in the falling of a sparrow or the flourishing of the lilies of the field in that blunt opinion. The death of God has been declared in every university common room. The glory days of the Kirk's influence are long since over.

The Presbytery of Wigtown and Stran-raer still meets in the hall beside Glenluce parish kirk, it being a conveniently central situation in this far flung shire. The Presbytery is the lineal descendant of those tough, stubborn Covenanters who opposed dukes, princes, and kings, but its adherents shrink in number with each passing year. Since 1959 the number of ministers work-ing in Wigtownshire for the Church of

Scotland has halved. If present trends continue, the Kirk will involve only a tiny proportion of the population. But that stage has not yet been reached in Glenluce where, on a Sunday, dozens of people of all ages still gather.

Beyond the parish kirk a steep road descends to the main street where, near the village hall, you will find a large display board with a map of the Pilgrim Way.

After Glenluce comes several hours of brisk walking before the next shop and hotel offer comfort at the little village of Mochrum. It is a wise walker who checks his/her provisions before leaving Glenluce. Wind and storm can brew up surprisingly quick to catch a traveller on the long, moorland miles, so adequate clothing should be packed, along with any necessary nourishment. There is another vital commodity for those who wish to experience the outdoor life of Galloway—insect repellent. This is a necessity: the Scottish midge has a voracious appetite. On a damp, windless day they can be a menace, especially in areas with standing water, bracken and trees.

The route now leads south out of the village towards Mochrum, past a stream in a little, wooded valley and up beyond a farmsteading where the flat, wide ribbon of the A75 Euroroute bars the way with the flashing metal of speeding cars. An underpass carries the walker or cyclist to safety at the other side where a small road winds over Barlockart Fell. This stretch of road is called the 'Clipper' by locals. It is a very ancient roadway that was once the main link between Wigtown in the east with Stranraer. It carries very little traffic these days, apart from occasional farm traffic. Grass growing up the middle of the road attests to that.

The 'Clipper' rises steeply until the entire length of Luce Bay can be seen sweeping in a great curve to the Mull of Galloway. Below, the Water of Luce spills its freshwater into the sea. The monks harvested oysters and great quantities of shellfish from the bay, and, at low tide, pools in the sand rewarded those with patience with a fine supper of flat fish.

Luce Bay has one of the greatest beaches in southwest Scotland with miles of dunes, pines, buckthorn and reedy, brackish ponds —a haven for wildlife. However, most of it is off limits to the public and red danger flags warn that this land is under the control of the Ministry of Defence. Air forces from Europe and America use the bay as a bombing range.

Another reminder of this modern age can be found on Barlockart Fell. Belching smoke and industrial noise reveal a crushing mill at the far end of the hill which quarries roadstone and concrete aggregate for the construction industry. The noise of the quarry is periodically drowned out by jet aircraft screaming overhead at little more than tree-top height to fire rockets at the targets on Luce Bay.

From flint-tipped spear to laser-guided missile, little has changed in human history. However, Christian Whithorn offered an alternative to the conflict of warrior societies. Peace, not war. Love, not hatred. Mercy, not vengeance and vendetta. Gentleness, stronger than violence. These were Whithorn's gifts to the Celts of Scotland, Wales, the Isle of Man, Ireland and beyond as this influence spread through northern Europe like ripples from a stone cast into a still pond. Peace is not lightly won, for it demands social justice and the protection of the poor against the strong. This, Whithorn achieved in great measure.

However, despite the crushing mill and the jet fighters, the 'Clipper' is a splendid place to walk, with its high, wide views of sea and rolling hills. The names of farms along it's way speak of centuries past. The area beyond Barlockart is called Kilfillan, meaning 'Church of Fillan' or 'Finian', to whose memory a roofless chapel was dedicated further along the shore beyond Auchenmalg. Finian was a sixth century scholar who had trained at Whithorn and worked throughout northern Ireland and southern Scotland.

The 'Clipper' eventually comes to a

junction at Kirkchrist Bridge. Kirkchrist was a preaching station of the Celtic Church for generations long after Finian died, showing that his work lived on after him.

The route now turns to the east at Kirkchrist, but a rambler armed with a map could be forgiven a diversion to the west down to the ruined harbour of Stairhaven, named after the earls from Castle Kennedy. One earl was the military commander who was held ultimately responsible for the Glencoe massacre of 1689. Rising to prominence by supporting the 1707 Act of Union with England and Wales, the family derived great prosperity from their Wigtownshire estates. Grain destined for a hungry Liverpool was shipped out from Stairhaven and cargoes of coal and lime from Cumberland were hauled from its wharf. Now the stone of the harbour lies tumbled by winter storms, like the once mighty ramparts of the fort on Cruise Farm. Coastal trading is now at an end with lorries and motorways having replaced schooners and steam puffers along the shores of Britain.

The nature of the coastline changes abruptly at Stairhaven. To the west are Luce sands, but to the south are high cliffs alive with kittiwakes and rocks covered with hardy and salt-resistant flowering plants like 'sea pink'. In Finian's day, Garliachan Fort, a mile to the south of Stairhaven, was home to the most notable family in the district. Built on a rocky outcrop above its own boatstand, Garliachan was a formidable structure with its stone and timber ramparts, a spear length tall, rising above thorn and bramble-filled ditches. From places like here, Galloway men, and boys, defended themselves against pirate raiders from England and Ireland. Perhaps it is not too fanciful to imagine that men from Garliachan served in the armies of the legendary King Arthur of Britain, struggling to keep the last surviving light from Roman civilisation alive in the west. He recruited his armies from among the Cymric Celts of Cornwall, Wales, Cumbria and southern Scotland. Arthur became a folk hero throughout the Europe of the Middle Ages, but behind the legend is the fact that a native Celtic war leader from Britain inflicted grave defeats upon invading armies of Gaels from Ireland and Anglo-Saxons from Germany in the century after the collapse of the Roman Empire.

You will note that every few miles along the coast to Whithorn there are similar forts.

Closer to Stairhaven than Garliachan is the Broch of Sinniness. Brochs were large, round towers built in Scotland from the second century BC until the Roman invasion in the first century AD. There is nothing else quite like them in all Europe. The height of a three-storey house, they are shaped like the water cooling towers of an

electricity generating station. Entrance is
by one low door. Inside, there is a circular
courtyard open to the sky. Within the
massive, thick drystone walls
was a labyrinth of cham-
bers and stairways.
Sinniness Broch
is situated on a
rocky causeway
at the foot of
the cliffs, with
the sea on three
sides. It has suf-
fered centuries of erosion, but it is possible
to discern its circular form and the
cunningly fitted stones of its low doorway.

BROCH,
33 A.D.

Impregnable to assault, brochs were
impractical for permanent occupancy. The
people of the district would gather there
only in times of danger—much of the
danger at that time coming from the sea.

Privateering Roman slavers made summer forays similar to later trading along the
coasts of Africa in the nineteenth century.
Chained captives were taken to foreign lands
and sold for commercial profit. The sinews
of the Roman Empire were powered by the
muscles of human slaves.

Sinniness Broch is actually the most
southerly of these structures in Britain. It is
a reminder of harsh and violent times, echoes
from which still reverberate in the roar of
jet engines.

The Pilgrim Way to Whithorn lies east from Kirkchrist, past the waterfalls of Milton Burn. The gentle sound of running water makes a welcome change.

If you have walked from Stranraer in one day and not rested a night in Glenluce or New Luce, the legs may be beginning to get weary. It is possible to follow a small road south from Kirkchrist cross-roads for two miles to Auchenmalg where a caravan site clusters around an old pub by the beach. This provides an excellent camping site for the enterprising walker who could rejoin the Pilgrim Way further down the coast.

Chapel Finian down by the shore is well worth a visit. It has a lovely well of pure spring water which bubbles in a stone trough beside the walls of this ancient place of worship. Pilgrims from Ireland used to land here before walking over the hill to where there was a small community of the Celtic Church.

The coastline here consists of a wide, gravel and boulder strewn foreshore. In the centuries after the Ice Age the sea level was higher, washing right up to the grassy cliffs that today are found several hundred yards further inland. A modern road has been constructed along the shore, but traffic is frequent and fast.

The route of the Pilgrim Way now moves inland, through a landscape almost devoid of dwellings. The northern end of the peninsula of the Machars is a country of forestry plantations and open moor with bracken, rowan, birch and heather vividly colouring the countryside in russets and browns in season. Peat bogs are interrupted by ragged rocks against the skyline. This is wild country, hunted by merlins, buzzards and owls, with ravens tumbling in the air, the singing of linnet and lark all around. Lithe deer share the pastures with sheep and the small native breed of Galloway cattle.

BELTED
GALLOWAY

At Whitecairn farm there is another great Bronze Age burial mound, suggesting that more people lived hereabouts over three thousand years ago than nowadays— so many members of the rural population of Galloway have moved to the cities.

After Whitecairn the tarmac road surface becomes a gravel forestry track. It is easily passable for walkers and cyclists, but impossible for all but four-wheel drive vehicles. The next few miles will be free of the sound of combusting carbon molecules.

Lochs dotted with islets appear through the trees. Many of these little islands were made by human hands piling timber and stone, laying foundations for small dwellings out in the safety of the loch waters. Called 'crannogs', life on these artificial islets would have been midge-ridden outwith the smoke reek of the thatched house, although safety from attack would have been a higher priority than mere comfort in dangerous times.

Some of the young forest plantations on this stretch over Challochglass Moor have been destroyed by fire. Gaunt, blackened stumps give a mournful view until the track climbs to reveal the great granite hills 20 miles to the east, rising behind Creetown and Newton Stewart, beyond Wigtown Bay which defines the eastern limit of the peninsula of the Machars. The Pilgrim Way eventually leads into these highest and most rugged peaks south of the Highlands and north of the English Lake District, but first the route has to swing south to Whithorn and the tip of the finger of land.

Kirkcowan village is regarded by many as 'out of this world' and lies to the north of Challochglass. A single track road runs south to Culshabbin. Waymarkers direct

A CRANNOG
LAKE
DWELLING

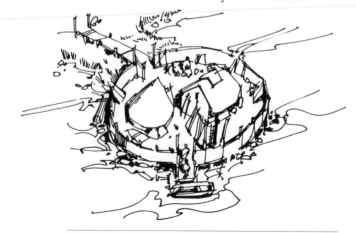

the Pilgrim Way to the south, past the
beautiful restored castle of Old Place of
Mochrum, before following the lapping
waters of Mochrum Loch. The towers of the
Old Place sit on the watershed of the peninsula. Mochrum Loch, beside the castle,
flows into Wigtown Bay along the Water
of Malzie and the River Bladnoch. Castle
Loch to the north of the Old Place flows
into Luce Bay along the Craignarget burn.
The road from Kirkcowan past the Old
Place is one of the ancient entrances into
the peninsula. It leads into the new lands of
Mochrum parish.

The place names of many districts in
Wigtownshire commemorate the sixth
century clerics who brought the religion of
Whithorn into the lives of country people.
Kilfillan we have already passed. Kirkcowan,
Kirkmaiden, Kirkmadrine, Kirkmabreck,
Kirkinner and Kirkcolm are all named after
individual divines. There is also a theory
that the whole wide land of Mochrum is
named after 'MoCronan'. The prefix 'Mo' is
an endearment meaning 'my' in the ancient
Celtic tongue. Cronan himself was the Ab
or Abbot of the ancient foundation of
Aoundruim in the Ards of Down over the
water in Ireland. Aoundruim dates back as
a place of Christian worship to the time of
the Celtic saints Ninian and Patrick—the
two peninsulas of the Ards and the Machars
had many dealings with each other. It is

possible, although very difficult to prove, that MoCronan of Aondruim had the same influence over this countryside that Finian had over his district beside Luce sands. The blessing these Christian men and women of peace brought to violent people is no mean achievement and is worth the memory.

At Culshabbin the Kirkcowan road meets a junction. The Pilgrim Way turns to the east, its way now blocked by Mochrum Fell which, at 646 feet, is the highest hill in the district. A stroll up the grassy slopes of the hill rewards the effort with its breathtaking view.

Opposite the disused school of Culshabbin a farm track leads towards the ridge. This track follows the route taken by pilgrims in earlier centuries. New horizons open up as the track climbs. South of Mochrum Fell the moorland becomes fenced pasture dotted with trees and hedging,with drystone dykes making linear patterns on the landscape. Whitewashed houses and farmsteadings provide a contrast to the varied shades of green. Mochrum Fell is three or four hours of good walking from Glenluce and this is a pleasant place to rest for a short while, where moorland russets turn into the greens of cultivated lands.

Incidentally, Galloway, at 55 degrees latitude, is as far north as the frozen waters of Hudson's Bay in Canada. At this latitude, also shared with Siberia, Galloway would freeze in the winter if it were not for relatively warm waters brought across the Atlantic by the Gulf Stream from the Caribbean. Frost is a rarity and grass grows for ten months in the year. The great farm machines reap tons of hay and silage for winter fodder, while salt winds contort the trees in all but the most sheltered locations.

Sheep and cattle thrive here. Farmers also grow barley in fields edged with walls built from the stones cleared from the thin soils of the ploughed enclosures.

At this latitude, the midsummer sun lightens the northern horizon on a cloudless midnight and the *aurora borealis* reflects off the polar caps. In winter, however, the days are short and dark, the air moistly cold. And, if it is a winter's day when you visit Mochrum Fell, with sunset early in the afternoon, do not linger on the hill, for the village of Mochrum is still four miles away and there may be no moonlight or starshine to light the way.

Some walkers may have avoided the climb up Mochrum Fell by following the waymarkers along the tarmac to Lochend of Elrig and there turning west to follow the loch to Elrig village. On this route stockyards and sheep pens found beside strong, stone-built barns are handsome evidence of the tough livelihood of farming. Sadly, such steadings are now being replaced by bland concrete, steel and corrugated sheds that look like any other industrial unit from Dusseldorf to Sheffield.

Elrig Loch was the meeting place for curlers in the nineteenth century who gathered on its frozen surface to hurl and sweep great stones in the intricacies of a sport which Scotland gifted to the world. Pundits pronounce on the dangers of ozone depletion and climate warming as a consequence of growing human populations and the use of fossil fuel powered technology. Only rarely in recent decades do the waters of Elrig Loch freeze thick enough for curling. So, what was an annual event, until as recently as the beginning of this century, is now sadly a rarity.

Behind the loch, tucked into a south facing fold of Mochrum Fell, are the wooded grounds of the House of Elrig. Its gables can be glimpsed between the trees.

These walls appear as old as the Old Place, but they are not. The House of Elrig was built in the years before World War I by the parents of Gavin Maxwell. Maxwell wrote the famous book

Ring of Bright Water, the story of the author's
life with an otter called Midge. This is the
countryside of Maxwell's childhood, and
otters still survive in the steams, lochs and
rocky shores of the peninsula. These days
they have to compete with packs of mink
descended from animals which escaped
from fur farms.

Gavin Maxwell wrote with a sensitivity,
a respect and sheer affection for wildlife and
the natural environment that was far in
advance of the huntin', shootin' norm of his
day. Perhaps the tragic death of Maxwell's
father defending Antwerp in the first
months of the Great War, and a fatherless
childhood in the bright new house his
parents had hoped to share, contributed to
the sensitivity of the man.

For five hundred years the Maxwell
family had a huge influence on Mochrum
parish. However, the House of Elrig has
housed only two generations of Maxwells.
The actual centre of their ancient family
lands lies a few miles to the south in Monreith. The Dalrymple Earls of Stair, Stuarts
from the Old Place, and Maxwells from
Monrieth once dominated the landscape
and its people from their great houses.

The first Maxwell came from the east
where the River Tweed marks the limits of
England. He married the heiress of the
McCulloch family and gained her lands,
establishing his name in the district. His

descendants became lairds and heritors, representing Galloway as MPs in Westminster.

When Gavin Maxwell's parents chose the site of the House of Elrig, they chose wisely. For others had selected the same sheltered corner centuries earlier. When Finian laboured at Kirkchrist and Garliachan Fort, when Couan built his kirk and gave the name to that otherworldly village, Kirkcowan, others settled and worked for the same cause in the southern sheltered fold of Mochrum Fell—where the House of Elrig is now. A local amateur archaeologist, despite lack of encouragement from professionals, recently persisted in a painstaking excavation of an early Christian chapel and associated buildings built within a turf enclosure in this same area.

The early communities of the Celtic Church did not build on the massive scale of the later Roman Catholic Cistercians at Glenluce. Theirs was a more domestic architecture of thatch, timber and mud-plastered stone, lime-washed to a brilliant whiteness. At Barhobble, whose name means 'hill of the priest', in what is now the private garden of House of Elrig, lived a community that practised the sacraments of the Christian Church until the twelfth century. This place was once a focus of community life as surely as Glenluce parish kirk was in its day.

The answer to the riddle of what caused

the decline of Barhobble after a history
twice as long as the Cistercians in Glenluce
becomes plain a few more miles down the
road at Mochrum village. First of all, however, you come to the two hundred yards of
Elrig village in a trim double row of houses.
Behind their gardens runs the stream from
the loch. At the foot of the village are the
remains of what was once one of the major
industrial centres of the Machars, up until
the time of the Great War. The roofless,
ivy-clad walls of a large mill complex were
built to use the steady flow of the broad
burn where it tumbled into a steep little
gorge. Sadly the lades no longer channel
the weight of falling water, turning the
great wheels to grind down animal bone,
imported from Ireland to provide sweet-
ening for the acid soils of Galloway. Scores
of men were employed here and iron-shod
hooves pulled clattering wheels through
the relative quiet of the village.

When industrial chemists in Germany
began distilling a new generation of syn-
thetic fertilisers at the turn of the century,
Elrig mill became obsolete and declined
into closure and roofless dereliction. The
waters still splash in green depths, but turn
no wheels to good purpose anymore.

Immediately beyond the ruins a Pilgrim
Way signpost points south to Mochrum.
This little road is a true rollercoaster, climb-
ing and dipping its way along the slopes of

Barr Hill. Sea waves ripple just three field lengths away on the tangled foreshore. The bouldered sea shore is adorned by cormorants drying their outspread wings and it begins to open up in a succession of small sandy bays among the rocks. In one of these, a large burn has dredged out a natural harbour where it enters the sea. Around this grew the little seaside town of Port William.

The Earls of Stair developed Stairhaven, further up the coast, to export cash crops of grain from their extensive estates. In the eighteenth century, the then laird of this district, Sir William Maxwell, had a stout breakwater built which enlarged the natural harbour dug by the stream. Around it grew the sizeable village of Port William, named after its enterprising Maxwell laird.

Like Glenluce the village of Port William offers shops, hotels and campsites

PORT WILLIAM

for today's visitor. The walk from Glenluce is long enough and Port William can be an excellent and friendly place for an overnight rest. A handy footpath cuts down to the shore from the Barr road.

However, Mochrum village is closer still, hidden behind the curve of the hill. It too offers a shop and a hotel. Mochrum's history is longer and richer than Port William's two centuries. Cyclists may well wish to press on further, but Mochrum is well worth a visit, even a night's rest.

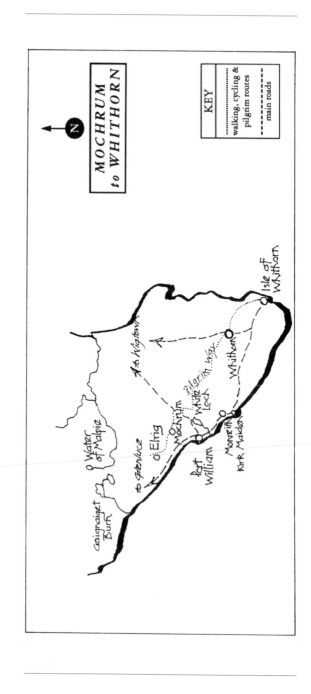

MOCHRUM
to WHITHORN

N

KEY

walking, cycling & pilgrim routes

main roads

Water of Malzie

Caigaiget Burn

to Glenluce

o: Elrig

Mochrum

White Loch

A to Wigtown

Pilgrim Way

Whithorn

Isle of Whithorn

Port William

Monreith
Kirk Maiden

3

MOCHRUM *to* WHITHORN

THE sea runs in the life-blood of Port William and Mochrum parish, though few people now earn their livelihoods from it at the end of the twentieth century. A small number of fishermen still catch dwindling amounts of shellfish, and others take out parties of sea-anglers, but the great shoals of fish that once swept through the Celtic Seas are much diminished. Overfishing, not so much by small local boats, but by steel-hulled vessels with radar and mile-long nylon nets have been a major contributor to dwindling stocks of marine life. The graceful, leaping porpoise have disappeared and the fins of huge basking sharks are now a rarity. Old men in the locality remember both species as having been plentiful.

Salt water has moulded the history of the Machars. When the land was a trackless wilderness of marsh and thick insect-infested forest, the first human inhabitants of Galloway made their arrival by sea. They were summer visitors who came by boat to camp on the beaches, returning to the warmer south when winter approached. They went back to their campsites on the

shores of Wigtown Bay and Luce Bay each
year until great middens of their rubbish
accumulated in their wake. Recent archaeological study of such middens reveals much
about the lives of these sea nomads living
on the Atlantic sea-board of Europe in the
sixth millennium BC.

The earliest written descriptions of long
distance sailing craft in the waters of the
Celtic Sea come from Roman military
reports in first century AD, and thereafter
from Christian writers in Ireland. Using
supple lengths of ash strengthened with oak
bracings, a framework was constructed,
narrow in beam and often twenty feet in
length. Ox hides saturated in grease were
then sewn to this frame. The technology of
such a building method, first recorded only
two thousand years ago, is in all probability
descended from the craft of the earliest sea-
nomads. Simple stone age tools and implements could readily construct a serviceable
hull with similar materials. Indeed, the
Innuit people of the Arctic build superb sea-
going kayaks and family boats using only
skins on a framework of bones, animal glue
and sewn sinew, and have done so for
thousands of years without recourse to the
oak and ash which grow so abundantly by
the shores of the Celtic Sea. In later times
metal tools would shape sawn timber into
larger, wooden hulls, but those first vessels
on the Celtic Sea were skin-covered.

Fishermen in small communities, similar to Port William, on the Atlantic coast of Ireland, still use tar and canvas covered *curraghs*, descendants of the earliest boat-building technology of northern Europe. Curraghs were swift craft, light to row. A small sail could set them scudding over the waves at a speed that brought the Machars into the range of one day's sailing from the coasts of England, the Isle of Man, and Ireland, when wind and tide were favourable. Keeping close to the shore and camping on land at night brought even Brittany on the continent and the Orkney Islands into the sea-going community of the Celtic Sea, although in such a light and fragile craft the sailing season would have been restricted to the summer months. In bad weather curraghs were light enough to be carried ashore beyond the dangers of the tide line. Upside down and weighted with rocks they created an excellent shelter against the elements.

Sea nomads in flotillas of curraghs brought people who gradually began to overwinter in the Machars as the climate warmed. Eventually these settlers came to learn the arts of agriculture.

Thus the human history of Galloway begins with the sea travellers. And in the centuries of the Celtic Church clerics made great use of curraghs as they developed international contacts. There is a persistent tradition that Celtic mariners reached Iceland, Greenland and Labrador long before the Vikings. An ancient Celtic prayer simply declares, 'O Lord help me, for the sea is so large and my boat is so small'.

The sea is still as vast as ever in Luce Bay, and at night, when the tide is in, the lights of the little town can twinkle off calm waters like the Riviera. It is different when the tide is out, however. Then, pungent odours from rotting seaweed in the harbour mix with those from the pig and poultry units nearby, whose low grey sheds dot the hill behind the town.

These animal sheds provide the greatest, single source of employment in a district where wages are hard to find. A recent survey has shown that the peninsula of the Machars suffers from being among the highest levels of unemployment combined with the lowest levels of average incomes in Scotland. Jobs at the pig farm are much sought after.

Pigs outnumber the human inhabitants of Port William ten to one.

Whilst it could be conjectured that the name for the wide district of Mochrum parish is derived from old MoCronan, the Ab of Aondruim in the Ards, there is another possible derivation of the name. 'Muc Dhruim' in Gaelic means 'pig's ridge' —suitable enough! However, the pigs of old Mochrum were tusked and hairy beasts, living free in woodlands, rooting for acorns and fungi, courageous before any hunter.

The road from Port William rejoins the Pilgrim Way to Whithorn near the White Loch of Myrton, and it passes by the squealing, grunting sheds of Dourie farm and its thousands of pigs in concrete.

Mochrum village is far removed from the reality of the Dourie, even though it is less than two miles away. Almost hidden by low, folding hills, the village is more properly called Kirk o' Mochrum. It is a place of ancient settlement.

Whereas Port William has the sea and the most glorious of sunsets, Mochrum is an enclosed kind of place. Its rows of cottages and their hedged gardens cluster around a beautiful old kirk that has recently been restored with the help of Historic Scotland, which also cares for the remains of Glenluce Abbey. Mochrum, however, was a place of Christian worship long before the Cistercians settled by their Water of Luce.

Like Barhobble on Mochrum Fell, the earliest church at Kirk o' Mochrum was built within an enclosing stone and turf wall. Fragments of carved Celtic stonework have been recovered, but the present kirk only dates back to 1794. Theft from country kirks in recent years has caused the locks to be turned against the casual visitor, but the key can be obtained and the inside of the kirk is well worth seeing.

The structure of the building amid its
ancient graveyard is shaped like a letter 'T'.
The downward stroke faces north and steps
lead up to the doorway beside its gable
end. Rounded Georgian windows give a
bright light to the interior. In the middle
of the south wall, an imposing pulpit rises
above a simple communion table on a raised
dais of polished wood. The interior is bare
of decoration apart from the rows of pews
and the capacious balconies supported by
stout wooden pillars.

The horizontal stroke of the 'T' is on an
east-west axis. This part of the kirk is
situated on top of the old mediaeval church
from its Roman Catholic centuries. At the
eastern end would have been the altar,
surrounded by candles and painted and
embroidered colour. It is in these mediaeval
centuries that the key which unlocks the
mystery of the disappearance of Barhobble
is found.

On leaving Mochrum kirk it is worthwhile making a short detour along the road
to the east of the village. One hundred
yards or so beyond the last houses rises an
immense mound of earth far bigger than
the Bronze Age burial mounds of Gleniron.
A deep, wide ditch surrounds it. This
Druchtag Motte is where a Norman knight
built a tower keep. Since 'Druchtag' is a
local Celtic name, it is unlikely that the
Norman managed to establish his family in

MOCHRUM KIRK

the district for any length of time. A
generation before the French Cistercians
were invited to Glenluce, Fergus, Lord of
Galloway brought Norman knights over
from France and England, like the one who
came to administer the lands of Mochrum.
Under his direction, local people were
forced into labour, carrying earth in wicker
baskets to pile high the Motte.

Fergus was anxious to have Normans in
his retinue. They were the masters of the
dominant form of warfare at that time—
the Cavalry. Booted and spurred, they rode
high in the saddle with the stirrup to brace
them on great stallions bred for war.

Armoured with hauberks of ring and
chain mail, their faces bore the stamp of the
cloven hoof. Their helmets with long nose
guards left pale shadows dividing one,
ruddy, sunburnt cheek from the other. They
were the most terrible killing machine of
their age and with mobile warriors such as
these at their backs, the Lords of Galloway

had little to fear from the pirate raiders who came by sea to rob and burn. Such pirates had been the plague of Galloway's coast for centuries. None had been more fearful than the Vikings, but even they were no match for the mounted, armoured Norman knights.

Although nominally acknowledging some kind of overlordship from the King of Scots up in Dunfermline, or in the border stronghold of Roxburgh, Fergus was as independent a prince as the Lords of the Isles in the Hebrides or the Kings in Ulster and the Isle of Man. By offering grants of lands to these tough Norman foreigners who had recently conquered England in the years after 1066 and the Battle of Hastings, Fergus was trying to weight the military and diplomatic equation in favour of Gallowegian independence.

Once the Norman Motte in Mochrum had been piled high and enclosed in a surrounding outwork of palisades, a simple tower of wood smeared in a layer of white-washed clay was built on the top, which dominated the surrounding countryside. The clay was not cosmetic, but a practical precaution against attempted arson by dis-gruntled locals who resented the Norman outsiders lording it over them.

However, the clean shaven, crop-haired Normans brought prestige to the Lords of Galloway in not only the military arena. In England, they already dominated the ecclesiastical structures that had evolved among the Anglo-Saxon kingdoms. Ancient abbeys, minsters and cathedrals were torn down by the conquerors and massive, new buildings erected. Fergus wanted to introduce this new fashion of ecclesiastical organisation to his principality, thinking it would increase his stature as a civilised prince in future diplomatic dealings. As a result of this Normanising policy a new kirk was built at Mochrum under the protection of the new castle.

In the centuries before Fergus, Galloway had been a battleground contested bitterly against invading Vikings. The influence of the continental, mainstream Church that looked to Rome for authority had never been very great in northern Britain and during the turbulence of the Viking centuries the involvement of Rome in far away places like Galloway became very small indeed. Nevertheless, native Christian worship persisted at places like Barhobble and

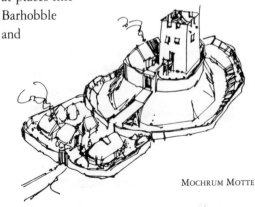

MOCHRUM MOTTE

Kirkchrist with the clergy of the Culdees,
or the 'Celi Dei', the friends of God, to lead
them. In Fergus's time the role of this
native clergy was to be usurped by
continental newcomers and their acolytes.

Mochrum Kirk and its protecting Motte
tell the story of the twelfth century attempt
to integrate Galloway more closely into the
European mainstream way of life. The new
kirk needed its castle because subsequent
new innovations involved the introduction
of Latin as the language of all liturgical
worship, in place of the customary
vernacular. For an unlettered population,
the use of a language they did not
understand would have brought confusion
and some resentment. Both Gaelic and
Cymric (Welsh) were spoken in Galloway,
with Northumbrian English coming into
increasing use in the coastlands—but Latin
thereafter was to be the language of the
Church.

One of the protagonists for change was
a fiery Irishman call Malachi. He had lived
among the Normans and knew and
approved of their ways. He established the
delightfully named Soulseat Abbey near
Stranraer, but he also visited the new
establishment at Mochrum. As this grew to
prominence in the district under the patronage of the Lords of Galloway, Barhobble on
Mochrum Fell correspondingly diminished.

For centuries thereafter, the village of

Kirk o' Mochrum became the centre of the local agricultural community until the modern age. Horses were taken to its smiddy for shoeing, and doubtless it was a place for chat and gossip. Conversation is still plentiful in the bar of the hotel in the village. This handsome house with its tall trees adjoins the kirkyard. It was once the minister's manse and its imposing size reflects the esteem in which clergymen were held in Scotland in the distant past.

The other significant building in the village is the old school. Now a dwelling house, it used to be a Youth Hostel for a few years after its closure as a place of education. Learning was once greatly valued, and the Church of Scotland was a pioneer in the attempt to create nearly universal literacy, girls as well as boys, throughout its parishes. The Reformer John Knox and his friends in the Protestant revolution of 1560 stated that a school in every parish, an academy in every burgh, and a university in every city were a priority for Christian Scotland. By badgering lairds and heritors, ministers were often successful in setting up parish schools and gaining scholarship funds to enable even the children of shepherds to attend university in Edinburgh, Glasgow, St Andrews and Aberdeen, at a time when England only maintained two universities and most of the population was illiterate.

Manse, kirk, school and smiddy constit-

uted the core of the life of Mochrum, as
surely as the old Celtic enclosure, or towering Norman castle, or Roman Catholic
church had done in their earlier centuries.

On the wall near the Greenmantle
Hotel there is a similar display board to the
one in Glenluce village. It shows the route
of the miles to Whithorn.

A winding country road through
peaceful-seeming farmland leads the way
out of Mochrum. Looking back at the
village from near a cottage with the name
'Sargeants', the village appears a sleepy,
dormant place resting comfortably in the
shelter of its little trees. Little suggests
another episode in its history involving
bloodshed and duplicity. It happened in the
eighteenth century, at the time when the
new kirk was built. Smugglers from the
Isle of Man brought brandy, gin, tobacco,
sugar, tea and coffee to the coasts of the
Machars. On moonless nights this contraband was stealthily brought ashore by
gangs of men. However, the government
stationed soldiers and excisemen in the area
to stop this illegal trade which robbed the
exchequer of revenue at a time when
Napoleonic France threatened invasion.
The clash between the soldiers and the
smugglers was sometimes violent and often
difficult with too few of the government
forces to cover the many miles of coast.
Furthermore, the local population were in

firm support of the smuggling bands as considerable profit from such a lucrative business went into local pockets.

When the Manxmen slipped away to evade the government sloops and cutters, the job of the local populace was to hide the contraband until a pack-horse train, sometimes involving one hundred horses, was organised to take the valuable merchandise up to Glasgow and Edinburgh. One enterprising farmer constructed a double cellar, one on top of the other. Non-contraband goods and tackle were stored in the upper cellar, dissuading soldiers and excisemen from searching further. Another devious and ingenious farmer built a secret storage room beneath the hearth of his lime kiln. When soldiers approached to search the premises the kiln fire would be lit. Quite what would have happened if a burning ember had fallen on a volatile keg of brandy is open to speculation, but the hearth and secret entrance were apparently well enough constructed.

The most famous exciseman to police the Solway shore was Scotland's national poet, Robert Burns. He generally worked out of Dumfries in the upper firth, but the cottage named 'The Sargeants' was a lodging for excisemen and soldiers deployed to confront the smuggling gangs. Kept deliberately at a safe distance by the locals, they were excluded from the secret, inner

life of the village which turned its back on
the government interlopers.

But enough of this—as the feet of the
traveller pace onwards, the eyes rest on
green fields with herds of cattle or sheep
who munch away like woolly maggots. The
herbivores of the farmlands have long since
destroyed the native forests in which
Mochrum's wild pigs once thrived.

These acres were once all owned by the
Maxwell family, but after the last War most
of the estate was sold. Many tenants bought
their farms and enjoyed for a time unrivalled
prosperity.

During the War against Nazi Germany,
Britain had almost been starved into defeat
by U-boat attacks. It became a strategic
imperative that Britain's reliance on vulnerable supplies of imported food should be
reduced. As a result government subsidies
were poured into agriculture and it was
thought that the mechanisation of agriculture and the use of chemical fertilisers would
increase food yields. For a time the benefits
of this policy were apparent, but it was
shortlived—the eventual, debilitating side-
effects of this technological approach to
land husbandry gradually became noticeable.

In recent years there has been a rundown
in the level of subsidies paid to farmers by
the European Community. Agricultural
income has been losing its race with inflation
and many farms face increasing difficulty.

Instead of paying the estate factor rent for their land, many have to pay banks large sums of interest on loans used to mechanise their farms under government prompting.

The introduction of threshing machines, tractors and combine harvesters into farming has profoundly affected life in the countryside. Agricultural labourers, their wives and families, those who earned their wage through manual work, are no longer required. Combined harvesters have made them redundant.

Many moved to the cities to find employment. Others moved to small housing schemes in the towns of Wigtownshire where jobs continue to be hard to find. Without the children of the farmworkers, Mochrum school met the fate of hundreds of others and soon closed.

There have been many changes during the last half century of mechanisation. One example is symptomatic of the many.

The writer Gavin Maxwell, during his childhood years at Elrig, would have been well acquainted with the call of the corncrake throughout the summer months. This little bird used to raise its young in the hayfields. The traditional art of harvesting was slow moving across a field, but modern farming machinery has killed off the corncrake in Galloway in three short decades.

A mile or so beyond Mochrum, the

Pilgrim Way joins the main Port William
to Newton Stewart road for a quarter of a
mile. The walker should take care—there
are fast vehicles on this part of the journey
until a quiet farm track leads through fields
and forestry plantations.

A very worthwhile detour can be made
near here. The Bronze Age builders of the
burial cairns that dot the landscape also left
mysterious 'cup and ring' marked carvings
on stone outcrops. There is a lot of speculation about the significance of these
detailed swirls and indentations. One of the
more plausible theories likens these designs
to the outline of ceremonial mazes and
labyrinths built and planted throughout the
ancient world as places for ritual processions
and religious observance. In the fields beyond Drumtrodden farm Historic Scotland
preserves some outstanding examples of
these mysterious carvings within strong,
iron enclosures.

From this vantage point of Drumtrodden
Hill a splendid view unfolds, with the sea
reflecting light from Luce Bay behind the
western rim of Barhullian and Carleton Fells.
Water also glistens from the White Loch of
Myrton within its surrounding woodlands.

Tradition insists that the White Loch
had healing properties. Skin infections, for
example, were soothed by bathing in it. It
was also claimed that linen washed in its
waters would naturally bleach to a shining

STANDING STONES, DRUMTRODDEN

whiteness. It is impossible to verify these claims because nowadays the loch is awash with algae which thrives on the pig slurry pumped onto the surrounding countryside.

The White Loch (or should it be the *Green* Loch) of Myrton was the historic centre of the Maxwell family's power and influence. Myrton Castle, which belonged to the native McCullochs who had survived the Vikings and Normans, was to become Maxwell property. When the family grew to a greater prosperity in the eighteenth century, they built the splendidly proportioned Monreith House that overlooks the loch. These Maxwell lairds also laid out the woodlands, among which are the largest collection of monkey puzzle trees in Europe.

We know for certain that this was a very special place for the Celtic Church. The tallest, most imposing of the carved stone crosses which now rest in the little museum in Whithorn once stood beside the White Loch. It marked a preaching place where bread was broken and the wine poured in divine communion. Outdoor worship among the fellow creatures of nature was a feature of the Celtic Church which saw the whole created order as suffused with the divine, the eternal breaking into the mortal with every indrawn breath. It was only after many centuries that Norman-inspired stone vaults were raised to hem worship behind walls, so that the call of the winter geese was no longer intertwined with the liturgy.

The road to Whithorn from the White Loch now runs through farmland enclosed within stone dykes. The soil is thinner here. Bare rock continually knuckles through and fields are scattered with stands of whin and broom. There is not a great volume of traffic on the road and the verges are wide, but it is always necessary to be alert for the sounds of approaching machinery.

The lovely woods around the loch end soon after the roadside lodge which protects the entrance to the driveway of Monreith House. Just beyond the lodge you can see two of the most imposing standing stones in all Galloway. Closer inspection reveals a third stone which has toppled over. We will never know what rituals and mysteries were pondered on this open hillside, but Bronze Age farmers must have dragged these stones here with the co-ordinated effort of many

—their purpose being to respond to the cosmic dance of life.

The waymarkers of the Pilgrim Way point down the tussocky miles of tarmac to Whithorn, two hours of easy walking away from the White Loch. However, there are alternative routes for the fit, adventurous walker who might wish to cover a greater distance in one day. Mapwork is essential in this case for there are no waymarkers along these optional routes.

First, you can follow the farm tracks west to the coast at Monreith. There the rocky jumble of the Machars along the shore of Luce Bay gives out to sweeping sand on either side of a promontory which is used as a golf course and manicured to an emerald velvet. Golf is one of Scotland's most appreciated contributions to the world, and this tiny nine hole course has a magnificent location.

Beside the golf links are the ruins of an ancient chapel with its surrounding burial ground. High bluffs behind the chapel are clothed with wind-twisted trees. In past centuries pilgrims came by land and sea to bathe in a spring beside the chapel. Tradition claimed that eye problems and skin diseases found a cure here—as they did at the White Loch. In the kirkyard there is a gravestone and bronze plaque—memorials to a terrible battle fought between French and Royal Navy warships in 1758. The dead were washed ashore and buried in this place. Graveyards in the Machars are full of those whose lives have been claimed by the harsh seas.

Beyond the chapel, round the headland, is a delightful beach favoured for family outings during the summer months, the air loud with the happy voices of children. The sand ends at the cliffs, the rockiest encountered by the walker since Stairhaven.

It is possible to follow paths along the deserted shore. This eventually leads to Ninian's Cave. Ninian, the first Christian bishop of Whithorn, is reputed to have used this cave as a place of retreat and contemplation. [However, please note— rare plants and animals only thrive when undisturbed by people, therefore it is best that this rugged coastline south of Monreith remains unfrequented.]

Meanwhile, the signposted Pilgrim Way passes more dairy herds and isolated cottages

ST MEDAN'S
CHAPEL,
MONREITH

ST NINIAN'S CAVE

as it threads its way towards Whithorn.
Accompanying dykes rise and fall over the
undulations like plates on a dinosaur's spine.
As you pass by the little township of Ravenstone and its deserted school, the Dutch
gable of a roadside cottage stands against
the sky on the final rise before Whithorn.
Breasting this ridge, a long, low straggle of
a town comes into view. The destination of
this day of walking, Whithorn, is now only
minutes away and weary feet may quicken
their pace with the anticipation of arrival.

A cyclist could make this journey from
Mochrum to Whithorn in a day, easily, unless the wind were unkind. A driver could
get here from Glenluce in less than an hour.
But the Machars have more secret treasures
for those who like to savour the moment.
So don't be in a hurry—or you will miss all
that the walker can discover at that more
gentle pace.

4

WHITHORN, PRIORY *and* BURGH

THE entrance to Whithorn, the most ancient Christian centre in the north, is prosaic in the extreme. There is little to suggest that this small town was for a thousand years one of the most significant focal points for pilgrimage in all of Christendom.

Pilgrimage appears to be one of the universals of the human experience. It is shared by every great creed in every continent. In Mecca the muezzin call echoes out to the faithful from minarets. The towering halls of Lhasa still beckon the brave and devout Buddhist. Terrible persecution by Chinese communists and the flight of the Dalai Lhama have not stamped out the ancient Tibetan custom of making a holy journey. Beside the Ganges temple courts fill with the annual throngs of Hindus searching for that contact point with the divine in sacred waters. Central to the Judaism which nurtured Jesus were the regular journeys from Galilee to the temple in Jerusalem. Ancient Greeks used to travel to Delphi to consult with the musings of the oracle. And, in the Christian centuries, international gatherings would flock to the great basilica of St Peter in Rome, Chaucer's pilgrims found an equality of purpose on the road to Canterbury and, in Scotland, places like St Andrews and Iona rose to prominence.

Closer to the focus of this book, remote Whithorn fascinated the imagination as much as any until the thoroughness of the Protestant Reformation in Scotland snuffed out the regular practice of pilgrimage four centuries ago.

Pilgrims made and make their journeys for many reasons. A desire for excitement and the simple stimulation of travel away from the humdrum reality of everyday obligations would doubtless have been motivation enough for many. Travelling lightly with only cloak, sandals, staff and satchel, the poor could hope for the charity of alms and the honouring of the widespread code of hospitality which graced those times. Richer travellers expected more and paid their way with gold and silver.

In mediaeval centuries the only other motivations for travel, apart from pilgrimage, were military or mercantile in nature. The main exception to this were the travelling scholars who were seeking new libraries in which to scan fresh parchment manuscripts, thirsting after knowledge above all else.

Pilgrims and scholars were no threat to the host communities through which they passed. They were not seeking conquest or commercial advantage. In the days before television, radio and newspapers released their avalanche of words, pilgrims also brought with them the stimulus of news and travellers' tales from far away places that refreshed parochial staleness.

As a result, a great network of inns and ecclesiastical hospices providing bed and board developed along the pilgrim routes of Europe and Latin, the language of the Roman Catholic Church became a *lingua franca*.

Minds from Scandinavia, Iberia, France, Germany, England and the Celtic world met in peaceful conversation as they travelled together on the miles to Whithorn. Their arrival at the burgh walls would have been a time of great excitement and expectation. Today the entrance to Whithorn boasts of none of the minarets, temples, or green cloisters shadowed by mighty towers that embellish other centres of ancient pilgrimage. Past the lorry-park where great vehicles are maintained after thundering down the motorways with Galloway cheese, beef and fish, a latter-day pilgrim, on entering Whithorn from the north, is welcomed by the thudding diesel generator of a dairy farm whose cows leave ample evidence on the road surface of their daily passing.

Whithorn is only slightly bigger than Glenluce or Port William. Upwards of a thousand souls live in a linear sprawl of two-storey terraces which follow the mediaeval street plan, swelling out in the middle where market stalls once sold their wares in a noisy bustle of activity.

This is the oldest urban settlement in Scotland. Its geographical situation, three miles inland from the safe anchorage at the southernmost tip of the peninsula at the Isle of Whithorn, provides evidence of the pirates who used to infest the Celtic Sea. Three miles of barking watchdogs would rouse the countryside and help thwart any hit and run, night-time raids.

For more peaceable seafarers from the south, however, the harbour at the Isle of Whithorn offered the first landfall on the Scottish mainland. Galloway had much to offer. Those intent on conquest and lord-ship over subservient peasants were drawn to this fertile land. The success rate of such interlopers with those native to the area was at best patchy over the centuries—a local saying has it that Galloway people are rather like their tough, local cattle: 'you can lead a Galloway cow,' they say, 'but you cannot drive it!'

The demands of commerce also brought olive-skinned men from the Mediterranean. The inland hills of southwest Scotland con-tained rich veins of copper, lead, silver and even gold. Phoenicians from the Lebanon, for example, traded with Cornwall for tin.

And many knew the profit to be found in an extra week of sailing in high summer to the land at the head of the winding Celtic Sea between Britain and Ireland. Animal skins, hunting dogs, and everyday goods like slaves, were also bartered for the wine, oil, pottery and cotton cloth of southern lands.

After the Phoenicians and their Carthaginian cousins from north Africa, the Greeks came, closely followed by the men of Rome who changed the face of the northern world with their iron-clad legions.

There is a lovely story concerning this time, associated with Glastonbury on the Severn estuary. Tradition holds that Joseph of Arimathea was accompanied by his adolescent nephew on a trading trip to Britain. His nephew was Jesus. Galilee was, after all, a neighbour to the Lebanon which had been trading with Britain for centuries before Jesus was born. Whether this is plausible truth or fanciful whimsey, the story does emphasise the antiquity of the trading links that brought international interchange to these most remote, islanded parts of the continental community—'and did those feet in ancient days walk upon England's pastures green ....'

Whether Jesus did or did not visit the site of Scotland's oldest town will never be known, but an undeniable fact of history is that Whithorn once had a railway which

linked the area with the Victorian and
Edwardian life of Scotland. Opposite the
dairy farm there was a station and engine
shed and beside it a large creamery which
daily sent churns of fresh milk to Glasgow.

The railway terminus and the creamery
are now rubble overgrown by nettles, and
the earlier international significance of the
town is no more obvious than the ruins of
Victorian enterprise and industry. One
reminder, however, is the heraldic device
on the sign at the edge of town—the coat
of arms of Whithorn consists of an angel in
a shining robe with the motto *Resurgence*
emblazoned upon it.

Iona of the Hebrides was once
Whithorn's twin in the religious life of
Scotland. After the Reformation its abbey
met the same fate as Glenluce and pilgrims
no longer landed at its white beaches.
However, in the past half century, the work
of Lord MacLeod of Fuinary and the Iona
Community has done much to restore the
island to its earlier role as a living focus of
the spiritual health of nations. The rebuilding of the abbey on Iona is a symbol of the
recent resurgence of that little island.

There are signs of a similar stirring in
Whithorn, even though the first church
building seen on entering the town has
been converted into a garage—petrol being
esteemed more highly than prayer it seems!

Where the main street swells to its

widest there is a centuries-old, whitewashed, stone arch. It is called the Pend and
it leads to the ruins of Whithorn Priory.
Beside the Pend is an exquisite, little
museum containing many of the religious
artefacts of past centuries. In 1989 a Visitor
Centre was opened beside the Pend, facing
onto the main street. There, in a comfortable theatre, an audio-visual presentation
gives visitors a 15 minute introduction to
Whithorn's rich past. Guided tours of the
ruined Priory and
the archaeological
excavations are also
available.

In 1985 the
Whithorn Trust was
set up to supervise
one of the largest
and most comprehen-
sive archaeological
digs ever to be under-
taken in Europe. It
has attracted many
thousands of curious

The ENTRANCE
to WHITHORN
PRIORY

visitors, most of whom drive in for an hour
or two and then drive away. It really is
worth resting for a night in the lovely
peninsula of the Machars.

However, anyone who has walked ten
miles or more in the one day will be glad
to rest in the town before embarking on
what could be considered the loveliest miles

of all to the Isle of Whithorn and Ninian's Cave.

At the Priory there is an information board like that at Glenluce and Mochrum. It gives the reader plenty of scope for a magnificent day of walking, away from the town to wild cliffs and the cry of seabirds above the sound of the waves. Holiday-makers who have driven here to see the Dig could quite easily enjoy this walk as it returns to its starting point after a circular meander—but it would be an incurious pilgrim who did not wish to linger at the Priory and learn from the discoveries of the archaeologists.

The oldest of the inscribed stones in the museum dates to around AD 450. It begins with the words 'we praise you, O God'. Sadly, the *te deum* of Christian worship has become drab tedium for many, but beyond the ruined Priory is the crisp Georgian parish kirk in which the Christian tradition of Whithorn is still maintained. Younger people in the community prefer to frequent the other 'kirk' with its petrol pumps and cheery staff. The sabbath congregation in Whithorn is probably at its lowest since the Vikings overran the town. It is all very different from the days when Kings of Scots, with their retinues of musicians and courtiers, would have walked bare-headed beneath the Pend of the Priory.

The traditional story concerning Ninian

and Whithorn was compiled some three centuries after the events included by the Venerable Bede of Northumbria in his famous *History of the English Church*. Bede tells the story of a young Gallowegian travelling to study for ten years in Rome. He was ordained and consecrated a bishop during his stay in the city. In AD 398 he returned to Galloway, resting on the way with Martin of Tours who instructed Ninian in the monastic practices which were then only in their infancy.

Ninian then established at Whithorn the first great monastic house in northern Europe beyond the furthest frontiers of the Roman Empire, but it was an empire whose defences were crumbling. Indeed, if Ninian left Rome in AD 398, it was only a dozen years before an army of German barbarians captured the city itself.

Bede wrote in his *History* that a great stone church in the Roman style was built at Whithorn whilst Ninian was bishop. It was called *Candida Casa*. Translated from the Latin, this means 'bright, shining-white house'. When it was further translated into the Northumbrian vernacular, which Bede spoke, it became *hwit herne* or 'white house'. There is a White House in the Kremlin and another in Washington DC, but Whithorn's is of greater antiquity.

Bede also tells us that Ninian embarked on missionary ventures which took him as far as Perthshire and the Firth of Tay.

However, the careful sifting of the evidence gleaned in recent years by the archaeologists of the Whithorn Dig has begun to paint a rather different picture from Bede and the accepted later tradition.

One of the main difficulties with Bede's account of the development of Whithorn concerned the Celtic chronicler Gildas who was writing in the early sixth century, a hundred years or so after Ninian, and two centuries before Bede. Gildas actually makes no mention of an early, major monastery at Whithorn and he was considered familiar with the shores of the Celtic Sea—it is thought that he was born on Clydeside and later lived in Wales.

The amended story of Whithorn's early history lays greater emphasis on a more gradual development which does not see a monastic community of any significance develop until shortly after the death of

NORTHUMBRIAN WHITHORN

Gildas in the mid sixth century, but not before.

Indeed the beginnings of Christianity in Scotland are not to be found in celibate monasticism, but in the study of Galloway's commercial links with Europe. Wherever there is commerce, military attempts of dominance soon follow. Rome, for example, extended its Empire into Britain so that it could exploit the raw materials of the island for the economic benefit of metropolitan Italy. Gold, silver, copper, lead, tin, iron, salt, timber, flax, wool, leather, slaves and many other commodities could be exacted. They did, however, experience some difficulty in the process, suffering a severe reverse in the Highlands, and they with-drew to establish a defensive line from the Solway Firth to the Tyne where they built a wall and forts during the reign of the Emperor Hadrian.

The influence of Rome did not stop at the static garrisons on Hadrian's Wall, but percolated through to greatly affect the inhabitants of southern Scotland.

In the Palestine of Jesus, the Roman administration used client kings like the Herods to rule sensitive frontier districts that were not officially integrated into the territory of the Empire, but which were thought necessary to control for strategic reasons.

It was the same in Britain to the north

of Hadrian's Wall. North of the Forth, Rome faced the implacable hatred of a people they called the Picts and the Caledonians. Between the Firth and Hadrian's Wall there lived three great tribal groupings— the Gododdin in the east, the Selgovae in the middle, and the Novantae of Galloway. Diplomacy, trade and the threat of the legions kept these three tribes relatively peaceful during the centuries of Roman power. As Roman clients and allies they were used as a buffer zone against the enmity of the unconquered Picts.

In furthering this policy of pacifying the frontiers of Empire, the tribal aristocracy of southern Scotland were courted assid-uously by the rulers of Roman Britannia. As a result, chieftains soon imitated the latest fashions of the Empire in their hill fort villages. The top hat and walking stick that adorned many an African chief when the British Empire was in the ascendant reflect the same process of apparent high status bestowed by association with the dominant culture of the time. It is thought that Rispain Camp near Whithorn was one of these half-Romanised aristocratic centres.

Outward symbols of Roman influence filtered through Hadrian's Wall, but other radical and more subversive influences were also spreading into these northern lands from the southern heart of the Empire. The ideas and literature of the new Christian religion spread as quickly as the contagion of a 'disease baccilus'—to borrow a phrase which Winston Churchill used to describe the spread of Communism after World War I. This is an apt metaphor, because the Roman military machine was ill-equipped to resist it.

From Syria, Iraq, Egypt, through Greece, Italy, Spain and into Gaul, Christianity crossed the narrow sea into Britain. This infant Church of the Roman towns was illegal and savagely persecuted. The first documentary evidence of the spread of Christianity into Britain concerns the public execution of Alban who was killed in Verulamium for his pacifist beliefs two centuries after Jesus Christ, his exemplar on Golgotha.

Alban was only one of many. Hundreds of thousands were killed in a persecution which foreshadowed the Nazi and Communist intolerances of this century. But it had the opposite effect from that intended —the once despised Christian minority soon became too popular and influential to be vulnerable and the traditional Roman State began to capitulate before it. The imperial establishment eventually abandoned its claim to divine status when the Emperor Constantine received the baptismal rite of Church membership in AD 337.

Throughout the ages, religious observance has been truly set on fire by those few people who searched the profound depths of the interior, spiritual world and saw its outgoings permeating the whole external world of nature, tempering even the terrible human potential for cruelty and selfishness, tempering it with the vision of a wonderful cosmic love.

Yet, on the other hand, religion has often been valued merely as the medium for a public parade of self-esteem and respectability in the eyes of conventional society.

The Christian Church, under the patronage of the Emperors, became very respectable indeed in fourth century Roman society, where it was admired as a great sophistication, the 'avant garde' of urban society. Perhaps to those who lived in the Roman influenced lands of the Gododdin, Selgovae and Novantae, the outward trappings of the new Christian fashion were valued alongside the glass goblets and southern wine—acquisitions which bestowed status on the Celtic aristocratic families who flaunted them.

Nevertheless, men and women with the spiritual fire of Jesus in their bellies did have cause to settle in the same areas, teaching the life of prayer, service and sacrament as practised by the universal Church. Therefore, both convention and conviction would have been present at the birth of the first Christian congregation in Whithorn.

The archaeological record allows that

Christian influence was developing in the
Machars of Galloway by AD 398 when tradition insists that Ninian began his mission.
Around this time, on the Belgian frontier
of the Empire, a bishop called Victoricius
began work among the barbarian tribes who
were threatening that part of the imperial
land. His work pacified them and the tribes
became federated allies of the Romans.

The end of the fourth century was also
a difficult time for the frontier in Britain.
The Picts had formed an alliance with Gaels
from Ireland and Anglo-Saxons from Germany, and their attacks against the Romans
had been incessant.

At that time Carlisle, at the head of the
Solway Firth, was a large and prosperous
Roman town with a resident bishop, who
would have been well aware of the achievements of Victoricius in Belgium. He might
have followed that example, sending a del-
egation to the Novantae chieftains. If the
Novantae could be bound to a closer loyalty
with the beleaguered Roman province of
southern Britain, Irish skirmishes in the
Solway could be greatly hindered.

Was Bishop Ninian part of a team sent
out from Carlisle? We will never know for
sure, but the tradition of Ninian arriving at
Whithorn on the specific year of AD 398 is
a strong one and needs conclusive evidence
to the contrary before being set aside. The
absence of proof is not the proof of absence.

So, whether a bishop called Ninian was active in the Machars in AD 398 or not, might be unanswerable, but it is probable that there were Christian people living in Galloway at an even earlier date. The archaeological record does not contradict this, but questions the establishment of a large monastery at so early a date.

Vows of celibacy in the Church of the last years of the Empire were not usual. Most clerics were married men—as was St Peter himself. Monasticism, after all, began in the very different conditions of the Egyptian desert, and the first congregations in Galloway had little contact with it or the outlandish notion of renouncing family life. Thus the early Church of people like Ninian would have been domestic in nature, and perhaps did not even have public buildings specifically set aside for worship.

It is interesting to note that it was not from Whithorn that monasticism in Britain first developed in the form which was to become so identified with the later Celtic Church. Rather it was the Severn valley of the Welsh which was to be the nursery of monasticism at the end of the fifth century. By this time, the long and sometimes successful defence of the towns of Roman Britain against the Anglo-Saxon invaders was weakening. Few urban centres fell to assault, but the collapse of trade destroyed their economic base—whilst war, plague and famine had decimated the population.

As in the first Italian monastery of Monte Cassino, Welsh monasticism was a response to the collapsing certainties of Roman stability. Throughout Wales, safe from barbarian invasion, hundreds of little monastic enclosures, similar to that of the later Barhobble on Mochrum Fell, spread throughout the valleys, and then overseas to Cornwall, Brittany, and Ireland. The influence of this new monastic evangelism in Galloway built upon the pioneering work of Ninian and the earlier, domestic, familial nature of religious expression. Only in the sixth century, a hundred years after the death of Ninian, did a great monastery develop at Whithorn.

Ninian's Church would have been very much in the style of the Roman province in Britain. His work would have been similar to the contemporary missionary activity of his famous colleague, Patrick, who established a Christian presence in Ireland. But there too it was not until a century later that the monasticism of the Celtic Church provided the impetus to turn Christianity from the faith of an eccentric minority into a giant force which transformed and gentled the Celtic world of the West.

However, during the lifetimes of Patrick and Ninian, tides of a different kind were sweeping over the Continent in the wake of Rome's collapse. The human population of

Europe was almost halved in some areas and vast expanses of farmland went out of cultivation. The framework of civil government, of tax-maintained law and order, of peaceful trade and manufacture collapsed in a Continental cataclysm. The only province in the West to defend itself with anything like success was in Britain.

The stubborn defence of the inhabitants of Britain over generations is remembered in the stories of a mythical hero king called Arthur. Behind the myth, however, is a more complex reality which is difficult to decipher. Arthur was probably a Romanised war leader who rallied the remnants of legionary discipline.

The reality behind the traditional story of Ninian is no less complex than the Arthurian legend. Archaeology in the acres adjacent to Whithorn Priory has only revealed monochrome shadows from a colourful and vital reality, but it shows that while literacy and all its benefits were destroyed over much of Europe at this time, Ninian's legacy at Whithorn kept the flame of faith and scholarship alive until it was fanned to a new brightness by the later rejuvenating monasticism of the sixth century, offering an alternative to a secular society scarred by generations of warfare.

Above the levels of the Celtic buildings at Whithorn have been found the remains of stately, wooden buildings in the style of

Northumbrian England. During the late seventh and eighth centuries, the bishops of Whithorn had to look to the Archbishop of York for guidance and authority in ecclesiastical matters. This was the age the Venerable Bede wrote about.

Chieftains, descended from the Roman-influenced Novantae families who first heard the Gospel, had been forced to accept the overlordship of Northumbrian kings—and a scattering of Northumbrian settlers co-existed with the native Celts in relative peace. This peace was shattered, however, when Vikings invaded both Northumbria and Galloway, leaving the area in ruins. Later, in the ninth and tenth centuries, Whithorn became the squalid wattle and thatched village of violent and illiterate people.

Eventually the Celtic chieftains of the hill country re-established their control over the peninsula and a Christian presence was re-established with a new line of bishops and the building of a great mediaeval cathedral for Galloway.

The rulers who emerged from the Viking maelstrom included Fergus of Mochrum Motte, and Rolland of Glenluce Abbey. Their independence was to be restricted by the Kings of the Scots who tried to integrate Galloway more fully into the national life of Scotland.

One challenge to the power of these Scottish kings was the historical fact that the English Archbishop of York claimed a metropolitan authority over the bishops of Whithorn as a result of the short-lived Northumbrian ascendancy over Galloway before the Vikings came. The Scottish royal court astutely developed as state policy the cult of Ninian, the earliest founder of a distinctive Scottish Christianity which thrived centuries before the English had a church at York!

After the Wars of Independence and the victory of Bannockburn in AD 1314, the English claim to administer the diocese of Whithorn withered. Eventually, Glasgow and St Andrews became Whithorn's ecclesiastical superiors—and so it remained until the Protestant Reformation rejected episcopacy and developed the Presbyterian form of Church government by committee.

Scottish monarchs over the centuries often chose to visit Whithorn for political reasons of state, demonstrating the ending of York's influence. But they were also human beings who hungered for the things of the soul. An aged Robert the Bruce travelled here, praying for a miracle to cure the skin disease which plagued his last years. Did that tough old warrior bathe in the White Loch or splash in the spring on Monreith Shore?

Going on pilgrimage to seek healing for physical and psychological hurt is an ancient and universal impulse most vividly

seen today at Lourdes. From the earliest
centuries of the Church, the bodily remains
of martyrs and other devout people were
thought to be full of healing virtue. The
sick and suffering prayed at the graves of
saints for the miraculous help thought to
reside in bones revered as sacred relics. At
Whithorn, thousands came each year to
touch the relics of Ninian—monarchs and
peasants alike.

Another Scottish king who regularly
visited Ninian's shrine was James IV who
was to lead his army, the flower of Scotland,
to destruction on Flodden Field. Ugly stories
were associated with him concerning the
violent death of his father during an up-
rising of rebellious nobles. Afterwards James
IV always wore under his shirt a chain
around his waist as penance and regret for
the manner of his father's death.

Shame and repentance for wicked deeds
were other frequent motives for going on
pilgrimage. Hellfire for the souls of the
wicked was preached by the mediaeval
Church as the eternal punishment after the
death of the body, unless people had sought
forgiveness and recognised the harm of their
actions.

In some ways, fear of hellfire as a means
to contrition may be a form of social con-
ditioning through moral blackmail. Torture,
murder, rape, serfdom, the horrors of
feudalism in which the poor often starved

while the rich gorged—all these and worse
thrived in contradiction to the teachings of
Scripture. Theologians of this pre-scientific
world proposed eternal hellfire to inhibit
the dark and savage side of human nature;
while those who lived kindly lives were to
be rewarded with the eternal bliss of heaven.

However, theologians also proposed a
third option—purgatory—which was presented as a state of being after bodily death
in which a soul could prepare for heaven
through the rigours and hardships of a
rather unpleasant celestial reformatory.
Thus many penitents, like James IV, went
on pilgrimage in the hope of earning
indulgences blessed by the Roman pontiff
which, according to belief, reduced the time
a soul would have to spend being purged
and cleansed in purgatory for sins committed in this life.

Robert Burns wrote the phrase 'to see
ourselves as others see us'. The judgement
of God on wicked deeds is central to Scripture, for 'God is not mocked with impunity'.
Perhaps God's judgement is in 'seeing
ourselves as others see us', when all rags of
self-conceit are stripped away. God's love is
no mere sentimentality, but a passionate
outrage against those things which bring
suffering to the poor. So Jesus taught, and
the prophets before him.

These aspects of mediaeval pilgrimage
—prayer to saints, belief in the healing

power of sacred relics, gaining indulgences from purgatory—were bitterly criticised as superstition by reformers like Martin Luther and John Calvin. They argued that the ancient practice of pilgrimage was a spiritual corruption deflecting the devout from the true, internal path of piety.

As a result of this Protestant scorn, the great pilgrim churches of Iona, St Andrews and Whithorn collapsed into decay.

But the dust and stones of Whithorn Priory, kirkyard and glebe still contain the memories of every century of the Church in Scotland, from its quiet beginnings, the years of its greatness, and its decline into virtual irrelevance when set against the priorities of a materially-minded society.

It is pleasant to linger in the quiet acres which shelter behind the old main street of Whithorn, but it is good also to follow in the footsteps of earlier pilgrims who extended their pilgrimage to the very tip of the peninsula where land, sea and sky meet together in an elemental starkness, and the soul is naked before the smile in the eyes of God.

5

GARLIESTON, CRUGGLETON *and the* ISLE

THE ancient road between Whithorn and its harbour at the Isle of Whithorn was called the King's Road because of its royal travellers. However, less important men and women have covered the same miles.

Today the ancient King's Road is no more. Until horses, and the farm labourers who worked them, disappeared from the land after World War II to be replaced by tractors, the countryside was full of men, women and children using their own two feet as they went about their daily errands. They were too poor to own a horse, a bike was a luxury, and new-fangled motor cars were not for the likes of ploughmen, stockmen, dykers and dairymaids. Thus the King's Road was frequented until these people were cleared from the countryside.

Since then, the route has become an obstacle course for even experienced walkers. Barbed wire has strangled the ancient right of way. Crossing points over deeply

excavated streams have been obstructed and plank bridges removed. Although marked on maps printed until recently, the King's Road has been surrendered to the demands of technological agriculture by public indifference.

It was the same for hundreds of miles of ancient paths and bridleways throughout Scotland. They had never had been tamed to the wheel, but co-existed with the traditional arts of husbanding the land until the requirements of large, agricultural machinery became paramount.

On the hill, behind a farm called Prestrie, the one-time dwelling of priests, there is a derelict stretch of woodland with the carcasses of dead trees felled by winter storms which litter the ground. Unlike the combed, clipped and dressed fields all around, this rough ground maintains its defences. Sheltering within the rotten wood are grubs and insects spared from agricultural pesticides. On these feast a variety of quick birds. The long, tangled grass is full of voles, and the thump of alarmed rabbits scurrying away from intrusion to dark underground lairs is heard all around. Moles dig deep nearby, nosing after worms. In the air above, hunting hawks pursue smaller birds and dive on rustling voles, whilst stoats and weasels kill to keep their frantic metabolisms warm enough to live. These sharp-toothed cousins of the terrible *wolverine* stalk their prey above and below the ground. Meanwhile, the hungry fox prowls for an unsuspecting dove, and cowering hare leverets hush at the passing of a stealthy cat.

All of this ferment thrives within the struggling, stretching chlorophyll in leaves competing for unshadowed sun. The world of nature is harsh with tooth and claw, with frost and drought, but it has room for a fathomless variety of life.

It is different in the lands subjected to modern agriculture, where thousands of giant cows, with udders swaying to a hundred-weight of milk, eke out the hours before the relief of milking. Bred to produce vast quantities of milk, these cows are often the product of artificial insemination, by which they received the genetic imprint of some prize bull living in a research station hundreds of miles away. The small, dainty Ayrshire cow, with its dimpled brown and white hide, has become a rarity. Its smaller quantities of richer milk no longer curdle the cheese of Galloway. Enormous beasts derived from Holstein and Friesland fill the fields, churning the entrances to fields into a soup of mud with their hooves.

A wise walker will not rely on the bull being in a shed hundreds of miles away. Great animals as tall as horses glower at the unwary from behind a ringed nose. The ring is placed through the soft tissue of the nostrils so that the farmer can lead and

control the usually docile beast with a rope.
Nevertheless, these giants are potentially
lethal, especially if an accompanying dog
has spooked cows with young calves. Then,
the instinct of a bull with harem and off-
spring to defend can give a walker the fright
of his or her life.

So, the King's Road to the Isle is no
longer a practicable or pleasurable option,
although perhaps a better form of agriculture will develop with less reliance on
machinery and chemicals, employing many
more people on the land. Advocates of
organic agriculture, who have long warned
about the dangers in modern methods of
farming, see just such a future. Perhaps
then even the King's Road to the Isle will
return again to public use and enjoyment.

Denied the ancient route to the tip of
the peninsula, a small road leads off the
main street of Whithorn burgh to the south
east. It passes Whithorn school. Whithorn
once boasted as fine and varied a library as
any in northern Europe. Scholars flocked to
study with the master of its shelves. Learning has a long pedigree here. Until quite
recently Whithorn provided secondary
education for its children. Now they have
to spend the best part of two hours in a bus
to and from Newton Stewart each school day.
The primary school remains, but the old
secondary school is used as a community
centre.

Whithorn has a very strong sense of community, and this is illustrated by the meticulously neat bowling green and pavilion. On warm summer evenings, tense and subtle tournaments are enacted in a slow-moving cheery rivalry with clubs from neighbouring communities like Garlieston, the Isle, the Port and Kirkinner. Champions of this gentle duelling compete before appreciative eyes and ribald comments.

The modern world has harmed the health of agriculture, the traditional foundation of Whithorn's economy. With the demise of coastal shipping, railways, milling, creameries and agriculture as major employers, there are few jobs in the district. Young people have to leave to find work, and the remaining population becomes increasingly elderly. But the ancient town is a sunny and pleasant place to live, where traditional decencies, easily lost in cities, still persist between neighbours.

Farewell then to Whithorn, royal and ancient burgh, cradleland of the Faith in the north. May your motto ring true as a resurgence of rural life, traditional decency, and Christian living are renewed throughout the nations of the Celtic Sea.

A stream accompanies the road out of town. Both meet again after the stream's meanderings at Portyerrock on the east coast of the peninsula. The road meanders too, between its Galloway dykes. A great standing stone from before the bronze age is incorporated into one of these dykes.

Portyerrock, as its name suggests, was a landing place for boats. When the swift ebb and flood of a Solway tide is surging at the Isle, on the exposed tip of the peninsula, against a stiff, southwesterly wind, it can be impossible to gain entrance to the narrow shelter of the Isle harbour. In such conditions a sailor can head for the lee shore of Portyerrock. Three centuries ago, when Whitehaven on the Cumbrian side of the forth was the third busiest harbour in England after London and Bristol, shipping bound for its busy wharfs from the Americas would shelter off Portyerrock until the storm subsided. To this day, huge bulk carriers anchor offshore to discharge cargo into smaller shipping that can navigate the treacherous sand banks of the Solway.

Red dust from iron ore often hangs heavy in the air over Portyerrock.

The Wigtown Bay coastline of the Machars is different from the western shore facing Luce Bay and its smashing waves and flurries of spume. For, on the east, trees and bushes grow right down to the high water mark. Nevertheless, the Solway has one of the largest falls and rise of tide in Europe. At low tide great ridges of layered rock stretch out beyond the pastoral greenery of the land. Ponds on the seashore used to teem with ribbon fish and shrimp in clean, salt water, among anemones and variegated seaweeds. While lobster, crab and other armoured creatures lurked beneath stones. Conger eels hid among the rocks beyond the low tide line and could be enticed to the hook by pungent, three day old bait.

There have been great changes in recent years. The Celtic Sea has become one of the most polluted waters in the world. Since it is shallow, the capacity to absorb poison is not great. Its entrances between Wales and Ireland, and Scotland and Ireland, are narrow, and the surge of cleaner, ocean water is constricted. Into this almost enclosed sea, an industrial cocktail of chemicals has been pumped to maintain the recent lifestyle of those who live in the west of Britain and the east of Ireland.

A more visible manifestation of this accumulation of industrial rubbish is seen in the disposable plastic which litters the surface of the sea and gathers on the foreshore, impaled on barbed wire, flapping in tatters in the wind, a mournful commentary on our times.

Less visible are the chemical poisons which filter through the gills of fish and every organism that used to thrive in the plankton-rich waters. The rockpools of Portyerrock now host only remnant populations of species that once were plentiful.

Another chemical plague threatens— when we burn wood we unlock carbon molecules that were placed there by the photosynthesis of plants. The wood we burn is rarely more than two hundred years old. When we burn coal, we release carbon from the growth of giant, tree-like ferns from the Carboniferous era of geological development. When we burn petrochemicals, we release carbon molecules of marine life accumulated on an ancient sea floor over millennia. This rich harvest of creatures died and sank to the seabed, imprisoned for years by sedimentation until the prospector's drill pierced through the crust.

When we extract energy by fission from materials like plutonium we release energy that was sealed away in the atomic structure of matter during an almost incomprehensible timescale. In comparison, this entire planet is but a recent arrival. The half-life of radioactive decay in substances which float about the Celtic Sea is 40,000 million years.

How the poison of more recent times got into this Sea is a saga in itself.

After the defeat of Hitler, Stalin's Empire threatened a similar nightmare. To counter this, the Westminster Government of the time decided to develop nuclear weapons as a deterrent to Stalin's Red Army. Top secret research by Government boffins was centred on the Solway.

At Windscale on the Cumbrian coast, and at Chapelcross in Dumfriesshire, bomb factories were constructed behind barbed wire. Their primary function was to produce fissionable materials. These places were military complexes, but they also pioneered the generation of nuclear electricity by using fission to boil up water to turn steam turbines. Immense amounts of dedicated talent and Government revenue were invested in this enterprise.

At first it was thought that electricity could be produced at very low cost for minimal risk—far less risk than that faced by coal miners. But initial hopes and idealism were thwarted by unforeseen difficulties and both Chapelcross and Windscale have leaked nuclear poisons for nearly four decades.

These emissions accumulate in the tissues of marine organisms and the effect on future genetic development and the reproductive ability of entire species can only be guessed at. Such is the reality of the modern Celtic Sea into which the little stream from Whithorn discharges its own load of toxic agricultural-based pollution.

To the north of this ancient landing place there is a hillside where some of the earliest sea nomads left an extensive midden. Imagination may conjure up the ancient campsite with its beached *curraghs*, and mothers and children tending mussels boiling in wild herbs. On a promontory of high cliffs is an unusual arch. Behind this masonry rise the rounded, granite slopes of the heathery Galloway mountains.

If a walker is content to remain for the night in the comforts of the Isle, a detour to the north of Portyerrock offers some of the most delightful walking in Scotland. Wigtown Bay is less wide, less deep, less shining than Luce Bay, and the land at the other side is less distant than the Rhins of the Mull of Galloway. The high hills of the neighbouring Stewartry of Kirkcudbright define a land distinct from the Machars.

The name 'Kirkcudbright' is derived from the Celtic way of pronouncing the name of the great Northumbrian bishop of Lindisfarne, Cuthbert. No other county in Scotland is named after a man except Kirkcudbright—'Churchcuthbert'. It is a rare compliment for an Englishman, and it stands witness to the great achievement of the early Church in taming the enmity between Anglo-Saxon and Celt, giving to each a common ground of values. The name 'Kirkcudbright' is a memorial to a great peacemaking, whose achievements survived the later slaughter brought by the Vikings.

An exploration of the eastern side of the Machars can begin by following the quiet road from Portyerrock to the little harbour of Garlieston four miles to the north.

Garlieston is named after Lord Garlies, a title traditionally held by the eldest sons of the Earls of Galloway. In earlier centuries the district was known as Kirkmadrine,

before the descendants of a side-shoot of
the royal dynasty of the Stewarts imposed
their imprint. The chief residence of the
Earls was Galloway House, set in wide and
beautiful estate grounds. It boasts as many
windows as Buckingham Palace and was
built to impress the district with the high
status of its inhabitants.

During the War against Hitler, the
then Glasgow City Corporation set up a
residential school in the grand, old house
for children evacuated from the horror the
Luftwaffe brought. When the Nazi Blitz
hit the shipbuilding and engineering
centre of Clydebank, the fires lit the sky to
such an extent that the glow was seen as far
away as Perth.

Waifs and orphans from soot-blackened
tenements, undernourished and sometimes
afflicted with rickets due to the effects of
the hungry thirties, learned to wield knife
and fork under the chandeliers which belonged to a nobility who had once thought
to live life as a separate species from the
universal poor.

The struggle against the Nazis, however,
made Scotland and Britain for a time, a
more equal and pleasant land. The prosperous officer learned to respect the ordinary
soldier. The genteel lady learned to care for
infants in ragged clothes. The idealism and
mutual respect across class barriers that
was generated in the hardship of the War

helped create the Welfare State and a very different brand of socialism from that promoted by Stalin.

Seen through railings from the road to Garlieston, Galloway House gladdened many a childhood and revitalised many a worn, city teacher. Although the school is long since closed, its exquisite gardens and arboretum are open to the public, and with them Rigg Bay of the golden sands fringed by the branches of mighty trees.

Offshore from Rigg Bay is a construction like an oil rig. During the War, mammoth floating structures of concrete were built from this platform—the Mulberry harbours which were towed to Normandy for D Day.

Rigg Bay, and the wider Garlieston Bay to the north, played a notable part in earlier wars. When Robert the Bruce led Scotland against the Plantagenet Edwards of England seven centuries ago, Galloway was the stepping-stone from which the Scots successfully campaigned in Ireland and the Isle of Man against English garrisons.

The Lords of Galloway had customarily swept the Celtic Sea with fleets of *birlinn* long ships. Scottish sea-power harried English shipping as far south as the Bristol Channel, bringing encouragement to bands of Welsh rebels to rise up against English dominance. Rigg Bay and Garlieston were the major naval bases from which this assault was made. Sleek hulls would have

lain beached on the sand as planks were
rivetted tight on the ribs of warships.

Pleasure craft and a few fishing boats
still gather in the harbour of Garlieston.
Out of scale with the domestic architecture
of the village is an enormous red-brick warehouse overlooking the anchorage. It was
used to store grain harvests until coastal
shipping removed the bounty of the
Machars. All such trade is now conducted
on the motorways. The only merchandise
in this once busy little harbour is the landing of a few boxes of fish. There are plans,
however, to convert the warehouse into
holiday flats. At least such a development
would bring new life and commerce to the
community.

Garlieston is a good place to find refreshment with its shops and inns. It also has
overnight accommodation for those who
might wish to tan under a warm sun at
Rigg Bay. Its waters on an incoming tide
over warm sand can be exotically comfortable. But for the traveller who wishes to
return to Portyerrock and continue to the
Isle, a coastal path leads round the headland
to the south. Butterflies and every form of
life thrive in dense deciduous woodlands,
and steep cliffs replace the sands of the bay.

The estate ground of Galloway House
ends at a tall wall with a creaking, wrought
iron gate. The path leads past a ruined, cliff-
top lodge from which the Earl's gamekeeper

menaced any would-be poacher anxious for some meat for the pot.

Beyond the iron gate, the woodlands cease and the lonely arch which was visible from Portyerrock looms only two field lengths away. These ruins are the remains of Cruggleton Castle, the mightiest stronghold of the mediaeval Lords of Galloway. The main keep of this castle was only battered into submission by the cannons of Cromwell's soldiers in the seventeenth century. It was then blown up with gun powder, leaving only the one standing arch. It had more successfully resisted other invaders before the age of gunpowder.

Cruggleton Castle was a fortified settlement when Ninian was in Whithorn. The independent-minded, twelfth century Lords of Galloway still had enemies enough to need strong walls on high sea cliffs. A tall Norman-style keep was built within the earlier earthworks and a wide, new moat was excavated on its landward side. Clustering around the draughty, stone keep, the soldiers would have been housed, and the saddlers, fletchers, blacksmiths, farriers, carpenters, masons and bakers who served their prince with their trades. All of this subsided into silence after the roar of the explosion which destroyed it.

From the eyrie of Cruggleton, the Solway coast can be seen running east towards the Pennine spine of England. The joy of this place is indescribable on a crystal, winter day. Snow reflects light into the sky from off the high, rounded roof of England, visible some fifty miles away. Closer, more dramatic and more powerful is the sky line serrating the Lake District mountains. The view of these peaks rising behind the water is Hebridean in its intensity. The one sobering thought in this wide exhilaration is the solitary plume of steam rising above the cooling towers of Windscale.

It is possible to follow the cliffs to Portyerrock. Stepping stones mount dykes in the field corners because many used to walk this way in the old days, but if a walker returns to the road from the Castle, one of the hidden jewels of the Machars will be revealed. On Cruggleton farm there is a curious enclosure with a wall encircling a copse of tall trees. When the foliage is in full leaf in high summer, it is impossible to see the outline of some of the most ancient walls still supporting a roof in the whole of Galloway.

Cruggleton Kirk was built as the private chapel for the twelfth century Lords of Galloway and their retinue from the Castle. It overlooks the tranquillity of a duck-strewn lochan. Though silent, it is a place which still speaks of the eternal verities. For the Lords of the Castle supported the integration of the local, surviving customs of the Celtic Church into the mainstream

CRUGGLETON KIRK

customs and usages of the continental
Roman Catholic Church. They supported
reformers like Malachi in their endeavours
at Mochrum, Soulseat and Glenluce.

Indeed 'Quicksilver Malachi'—the
protagonist of the new and the antagonist
against time-honoured, local custom—
would have applauded the design of
Cruggleton Kirk. With the chancel of the
ordained separated from the nave of the
laity, it was suitable for the Roman liturgy.
The mediaeval Kirk of Mochrum was in all
probability very similar, but Cruggleton
Kirk, unlike its castle, escaped demolition
and its outlines were not obscured by the
rebuilding of a more spacious, presbyterian
place of worship.

When the Castle was destroyed, its
human community was dispersed.
Associated with the royalist aristocracy
who had tried to enforce the king's bishops
on the populace, Cruggleton Kirk lost the

affections of the ordinary country people. It
was never a centre of presbyterian parish
life after that. Instead, the little village of
Sorbie, some three miles inland, gained that
honour and so Cruggleton was left to moul-
der in its fields.

It was re-roofed and saved from dereliction by a Victorian philanthropist and is now
owned by the local farmer who happily and
generously encourages people to visit. The
farmer's wife looks after the key to the fine,
old oak and iron studded door.

The kindness of this family is heart-
warming. It was an ancient tradition that
those pilgrims who could do so, made a gift
offering, so why not make a gift to a charity,
any charity, after enjoying the freely-given
treasure of the Kirk?

The modern visitor to the Kirk will
enter a dark cavern where shafts of light
pierce through high, narrow windows.
Infinity still reverberates within its stillness,
and there are echoes of the life of Nazareth
lived in Galloway in emulation of distant
Galilee. When a prince's court gathered in
this place to worship, the interior would
have been carefully plastered and brightly
decorated with carved and gilded wood,
furnished and painted to create a place in
which candles, incense and chanting would
have mingled before the majesty of divine
rites. Only bare, rough stonework remains.

The road beyond the Kirk swiftly leads

to Portyerrock, and the Pilgrim Way to the Isle. For those who still have a spring in their step, it is possible to follow the coast around the headland beyond Portyerrock. But for the weary, it is only a short half hour along the tarmac.

The headland path is lonely with only the cry of seabirds for company. Stiff-winged kittiwakes turn in the air among more graceful terns, and gannets dive in a flash of yellow and ivory into shoals of fish. The coastline veers westward and the sea is deprived of the shelter of land when the Isle of Whithorn comes into view.

The Isle is no longer an island. A causeway has been built to create a narrow isthmus. It was constructed by Sir John Reid, Laird of the Isle, two centuries ago. He was the commanding officer of a government sloop during the campaign to suppress smuggling, and the building of the causeway came soon after a rather embarrassing incident.

A smuggler's vessel had been intercepted by the fast, heavily armed government sloop out on patrol in Luce Bay. Both vessels raised every inch of available canvas. It was a race in deadly earnest as spars, mast and rigging thrummed with the strain. Running before wind and tide, both vessels travelled at a speed which amazed onlookers on the shore. Cannon were run out, and shot and powder made ready as Sir John's sloop began to gain on the smuggler. Blood was sure to flow—as it did when the French were cornered by the Royal Navy off Monreith—unless the smuggler surrendered. Suddenly, off the Isle, the smuggler dipped his sails and meekly appeared to enter the shelter of the anchorage. Sir John and his crew were relieved—they had gained a rich prize without bloodshed. But on entering the harbour, satisfaction soon turned to dismay when they found their quarry standing out to sea again and making for the safety of the Isle of Man.

On the day of the chase there had been an unusually high tide and the canny skipper of the smuggler had driven his smaller vessel over the shingle bank at the head of the Isle harbour which was only drowned at high tide. The draught of the government cutter was too great to risk the chase, and it was impossible to beat against the wind the way they had come.

When low tide came, it could be seen that a great furrow had been gouged out of the shingle by the escaping keel.

Sir John would not be shamed that way again. Thus the causeway was built and a terrace of houses built upon it.

Half way along, on the harbour side and projecting below the high water mark, an unusual, whitewashed kirk has been built on carefully piled foundations. The reason behind this extraordinary architecture was a crisis which developed in the presbyterian idealism of the Church of Scotland.

The origins of the religious renaissance of the Protestant Reformation were in the great trading cities of northern Europe. The *coup d'état* of 1560 banished the influence of the Roman Catholic royal court of France from Scotland. The 'Auld Alliance' was ended and a new community of interest with Protestant England was established.

The main influences on the Scottish Reformation, however, came from the continent. Amsterdam, Geneva, Copenhagen, Hamburg and Strasbourg were manufacturing and mercantile centres in which guilds of craftsmen and traders gained freedom through their wealth from a countryside which was still dominated by feudal knights and barons.

The hierarchy of the Roman Catholic system of ecclesiastical administration had developed throughout the Middle Ages, parallel to the secular feudalism which dominated a peasantry reduced to serfdom. The presbyterian form of ecclesiastical administration through representative committees had more in common with urban craft guilds and councils of burghers than with the feudal baronage or the equivalent hierarchies of bishops, metropolitan archbishops, legates and cardinals.

These new ideas were transported to Scotland by John Knox and his friends.

Aberdeen, Perth, Dundee and Edinburgh readily grasped the urban lead of these continental innovations. Malachi and Knox would probably have found much in common, both being committed reformers who wished to banish introverted conservatism from the Church in their different centuries; but a thriving Hanseatic League city like Lubeck on the Baltic coast was a very different proposition from rural Scotland when it came to the implementation of the idealism of Martin Luther and John Calvin.

Feudalism was rarely as brutal in Scotland as it became elsewhere. The Continental Normans did not come to Scotland as conquerors as they did to England. Instead they came as well-paid mercenaries who inter-married with the native Celtic aristocracy.

Ties of kinship and a fascination for genealogies over many generations blurred the division between peasantry and nobility. And burgh councils in the urban centres of Scotland stopped any domination of the new presbyterian Church by rural aristocrats.

But in country areas it was different. There, the gentry expropriated the lands of the old Roman Catholic Church. In return they undertook to maintain the Protestant ministers with stipend, manse, glebe and kirk. The moral authority of the Church of Scotland was sufficient to keep most lairds and heritors up to their obligations; and in years when harvest failed, parish ministers were able to exact resources for the relief of the hungry from the new landowners—it is a true saying that 'he who pays the piper calls the tune'.

One of the fundamental ideals of the presbyterian form of ecclesiastical administration was the right of a congregation in a parish to choose its minister by a free vote. Heritors and lairds saw it otherwise, and the system of patronage whereby only the heritable landowners chose the minister, began to infiltrate and subvert the wishes of the founding fathers of the new Church.

The process aroused indignant opposition and breakaway groups established independent congregations throughout the eighteenth century. In 1843 the matter came to a crisis in what was thereafter called the Disruption. Half the ministers of the established Church of Scotland left to form the Free Kirk which renounced the right of the gentry to choose parish ministers.

The later theology of Free Presbyterianism has in recent years been mocked for narrow-minded and killjoy attitudes, and has been censured for bigotry against Roman Catholicism—but the Disruption in many ways showed presbyterianism at its most democratic and egalitarian best.

Most Free Kirk congregations rejoined the Church of Scotland in 1929. They had made their point successfully about the corrupting influence of the patronage of the rich over the rights of the poor in the governing of the Christian Church. However, in the Highlands and Islands, some Free Presbyterians remained aloof and separate.

The recent mechanisation of farming has cleared most of the labouring population from the farms of the Machars of Galloway, but there had been far more terrible evictions in rural Scotland during the previous two centuries. In the Highlands and Islands of the north, the clans were ruthlessly cleared for sheep. Unconquered by Romans, Vikings, Normans and English, the clans of the north were destroyed by the commercial urge to establish sheep-ranching.

Refugees fled to face cholera and typhoid in a Glasgow more like Calcutta than the douce city of today. The population exploded from the little university city with its salmon fishery at the time of the 1707 Act of Union with England and Wales, to the megalopolis that built the steel ships for half the world, in the coal-grimed city of a million people, twinkling with the electric lights which illuminated the trams in 1907.

The influx of rural refugees to hardship similar to that suffered by Third World refugees today ensured that more people died in Glasgow during the Clearances than were born in the city in the years leading up to the Disruption.

Other weary exiles were herded onto overcrowded 'coffin ships' bound for Canada and the United States. It was a terrible premonition of what would soon befall the Irish after their potato famine. They too would take 'coffin ships' across the Atlantic. They too would arrive destitute on the Glasgow docks.

To make matters worse, in the Highlands and Islands many ministers were little more than the mouthpiece of the lairds and chieftains who set ancient family loyalties as very little in comparison to the profit to be gained from sheep-ranching. Cash-crop agriculture supplanted the subsistence husbandry of the people. These patronage ministers stood back and watched the destruction of the people of the land as they were evicted from their holdings. Some even preached on Old Testament texts, telling how God had driven the Israelites from the milk and honey of Canaan, allowing their defeat by Assyrians and Babylonians because they had become an unrighteous people accursed of God.

It is no wonder that Free Presbyterianism still has the loyalty of many adherents in the north. Its ministers spoke bravely and without inhibition against the cruel greed of the rich.

The bitterness of the legacy of the Clearances is illustrated by this story from the Crimean War in 1854, only a decade after the Disruption. Recruiting sargeants entered the Highlands expecting to raise regiments as magnificent as those which had defeated Napoleon and subjugated India. Everywhere they went among the townships of the remaining croftlands, the sargeants heard the same refrain: 'you preferred sheep to men. Let sheep defend you, then!'

Clearances were not only a thing of the north. Galloway suffered in the eighteenth century. The agriculture of the peasants using strip cultivation in run rig fields ended when lairds enclosed the common pastures and stopped the age-old grazing rights of the peasants. Enclosure and the development of cash-crop agriculture by the lairds brought ruin to a lot of poor Galloway farmers. Many went to Northern Ireland and from there to America. Rebellious Galloway 'levellers' used to knock down the new stone dykes and uproot hedges, but the rich and powerful succeeded in their plans. After all, they had the lawyers and the courts to back them.

The Earls of Galloway exerted great patronage in the Machars. Tenant farmers on the kirk session of Sorbie parish did not thwart their landlord when he closed their much loved Sorbie kirk against the wishes of the congregation. This forced a move to a site more convenient for Galloway House where he built a grand, gothic structure with stained glass and every Victorian embellishment you can think of.

But others were not so easily led as that kirk session of Sorbie. At the Isle, a Free Kirk congregation gathered and turned their backs on the heritor-dominated cliques in Whithorn and Glasserton parishes. In time this new congregation had finances sufficient to buy timber, slate, glass and plaster. They employed carters to haul in stone and mortar, but no landowner in the district would sell ground on which the Free Kirk could build its house of public worship. So they built their simple kirk out into the Isle harbour, raising it above the seaweed as a testament to the age-old struggle of the poor against the rich.

Beyond the kirk at the end of the causeway is an irregular timber building which appears to be slowly collapsing in crazy

FISHING BOATS, ISLE OF WHITHORN

angles. It is a shop containing delights for the weary. The Isle also has several bed and breakfast establishments and there is a good Inn. A mile or so outside the village is a campsite on Burrow Head.

A favourite resting place is beside the fire in the bar of the Steampacket Inn. A wide window opens out on the harbour, with plate glass to keep chill winds at bay. These winds rattle through the rigging in a flotilla of sailing boats, taught wire drums against alloy masts. Sturdier and more workmanlike are the hulls of the fishing boats that still work out of here. As the Steampacket Inn name suggests, Victorian steamers took passengers from this dock-side bound for Liverpool, Dublin and the Isle of Man. The building of the railway to Whithorn, however, ended the excitement of passengers thronging the harbour.

Raising a glass with fresh froth to the brim and dew misting the rim, it is good to toast the golden miles of Galloway.

'He who loves not wine, wife and song, remains a fool all his life ...'
~ MARTIN LUTHER ~

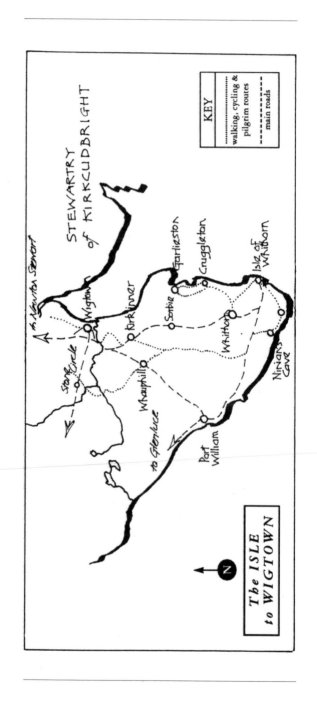

The ISLE to WIGTOWN

N

KEY
.... walking, cycling & pilgrim routes
- - - - main roads

to Newton Stewart

STEWARTRY of KIRKCUDBRIGHT

Stone Circle

Wigtown

Kirkinner

Whauphill

to Glenluce

Sorbie

Garlieston

Cruggleton

Whithorn

Isle of Whithorn

Port William

Ninian's Cave

6

The ISLE
and the CAVE

BEYOND the Steampacket Inn lies a tidal island of a few sparse acres. Its thin soil and tussocky hummocks of grass fail to hide the underlying rock. Pilgrims from overseas gave thanks for safe arrival in a small church on the island. The arch of the glassless window at the Jerusalem end looks out onto waves and a watery horizon. In Spring and Autumn the dawning sun shines through this window when dawn begins to flood the Machars with spectrums of light reflecting off the Solway. It must have been wonderful inside this building at such times, when the kirk was more than a roofless ruin. During the morning liturgies the new light would have shone through coloured glass to flood the interior with fire.

The earliest name associated with Ninian's first settlement three miles inland was *Candida Casa*. This name was translated into the Northumbrian *Whithorn* or 'White House'. However, *Candida* has a different meaning from the Latin word *alba* which means 'white'. In fact, *Candida* was a special word most commonly used to describe the lustre of a new, shining, bright toga; the white garment of aristocrats. It was the word which Jerome, the translator of the first Latin Bible, used to describe the transfiguration of Jesus.

Perhaps the name *Candida Casa* referred to the shining, spiritual nature of Ninian's settlement more than to the architectural qualities of the building Bede noted as *Hwit herne*. The 'Shining Place' is indeed a good description, a good translation for *Candida Casa*. The little kirk on the Isle, built in Ninian's honour, would have had a welcome shining through its eastern window for many a traveller. However, it is more difficult to imagine these things if it is a cold, grey day.

On the last rise of land beyond the kirk there is a small whitewashed tower, a marker for those arriving by sea. Some enthusiasts in the local sailing club wanted to paint it bright luminous orange so that it would be even more visible to mariners. The idea was quietly dropped, however. Beside the tower are some benches on which to sit and ponder the ending of solid land and the beginning of the watery world. On Iona they say:

> *deep peace of the flowing air to you,*
> *deep peace of the running wave to you,*
> *deep peace of the quiet earth to you,*
> *deep peace of the shining stars to you,*
> *deep peace of the Prince of Peace*
> *be upon you.*

The peace of mind which passes understanding is the gift of heaven to all pilgrims of
good will, no matter their race or creed—
love knows her own.

On the night before the judicial murder
of Jesus, after the bread and the wine, the
carpenter who only owned what he stood
up in gave his friends the most precious
gift this world offers—the peace which
passes understanding, which brings the life
of Nazareth to everywhere, even to these
hard rocks where Galloway is overwhelmed
by the sea. Peace brings hope to overwhelm
everything that threatens to bring misery.

Leaving the white tower of the Isle, the
path goes over the moat and ditches which
fortified this strategic speck of land when
Ninian lived. Just before the harbour and
causeway there is a steep ramp down which
the volunteer crew of the local lifeboat used
to plunge to rescue those in danger on the
sea. The bravery and compassion of the
fishermen of the Isle on countless occasions
was not so different from that of the fishermen friends of Jesus.

The only lifeboat in the Scottish Solway
is now in Kirkcudbright harbour, although
smaller inflatables are still worked by local
volunteers and coastguards. It is always a
saddening sight to see these fast boats,
usually accompanied by a military heli-
copter, quartering the sea: Is someone in
peril and a family tragedy in the making?

The hope of heaven, the peace of mind, is a gift which has made gentle Galilean and Gallowegian fishermen as brave as any soldier.

The Isle of Whithorn smells pungently of seaweed at low tide, though not quite in the same league as the mile-wide odours of Port William. Even so, the inlet on the eastern side of the causeway collects great mounds of seaweed which rot in the weeks that follow. Locals call it the 'stinking port', for the tide no longer surges over the shingle to sweep it clean because the causeway forms a barrier.

The Pilgrim Way leads out of the village on a green, farm track following the shore. The cliffs grow taller and more terrible. Down below where the waves seethe and boil are fangs of jagged rock, and further inland there rises the hump of the Howe Hill of Haggagmalag— 'Malachi's hill'. Burrow Head is the uttermost tip of the peninsula. Above its sheer cliffs was built one of the most impressive pre-Christian fortified camps in southern Scotland. Its situation is certainly imposing. A careful eye can discern the deep ditches and banks which enclosed an area of more than 15 acres.

This Celtic fortress was built on a larger scale than the domestic fortlet of Garliachan at Stairhaven. Dozens of round houses would have made a township within turf, timber and stone ramparts, hedged about with thorns, nature's barbed wire.

At the time when Jesus was hung on the tree of Golgotha, Britain was at war with itself, as tribes clashed for dominance and control over stretches of life-giving farm and hunting land. Just as foxes drive others away from the locality in which they hunt, and robins fight bloody battles for control of back gardens, every individual of every species is in a life or death competition for food. They either compete as individuals or band together in herds and packs. Human history shows that we are no different, except that the pack extended into the clan, the tribe, the nation and ultimately the empire in rivalry with other imperial ambitions.

Each development of human ingenuity has enabled more food to be produced and a time of peace and plenty would ensue. For example, the development of agriculture led to an explosion of the human population and the use of iron implements brought more land to the plough.

But when a human population reached the limits of its ability to feed itself, strains and tensions developed until widespread tribal aggression was the result. That stage had been reached among the tribes of Celtic Britain—at the time when Jesus Christ was riding in triumph into Jerusalem on the back of a donkey.

The most terrible tribe in northern
Britain at that time were the Brigantes of
what is now Yorkshire, Lancashire, West-
moreland, Cumberland and Durham. The
modern word 'brigand' still carries a vague
echo of their terror. Even Rome's invincible
legions struggled for decades to break their
spirit.

There is a theory which explains why
the Novantae, Gododdin and Selgovae of
southern Scotland did not make war upon
the Roman Empire—the disciplined legions
were in fact rescuing them from Brigantian
attacks. And these enemies of the people
who built the fort on Burrow Head also
came from Ireland as well as from the lands
of the Brigantes.

Beyond the ancient fortification from
that age of tribal warfare, lies Burrow Head
caravan site. On the Continent, city dwell-
ers often build little cabins of wood, brick
and tile in the countryside for weekend
retreats. Some, like the Czechs and Danes,
build delightful little townships of holiday
cabins surrounded by allotments of fruit and
flowers. In Britain the tendency has been to
buy factory-made caravans, metal sheeted
and brightly painted. Dozens of these
little boxes dot the bare hillside beyond
Burrow Head. In the weeks of summer, city
children run barefoot on the grass.

The caravan site used to be a military
base. Huge guns from obsolete battleships

were hauled up the hill and mounted in concrete bastions during World War I. The theory was that projectiles from these guns would close the narrow waters between the Machars and the Isle of Man to enemy shipping. U-Boats of the Imperial German Navy, however, rendered the guns useless.

At the close of World War II, thousands of defeated soldiers from the Nazi armies were brought to prisoner-of-war camps in Scotland. Young boys and men from the Ukraine, Austria, Croatia, Slovakia, Hungary, Italy and Germany were brought here, facing an uncertain future. Many ended up behind the barbed wire of Burrow Head.

Prisoners of the Soviet Union faced death through brutality, cold, hunger and overwork in Stalin's Gulag. The French and Americans allowed hundreds of thousands of prisoners of war to die in unheated sheds on a diet of thin gruel in the bitter winter which followed 1945. It was a terrible episode of hushed-up, deliberate policy, designed to break the fighting spirit of the German soldier. It is as shameful as the bombing of undefended cities full of refugees in the closing months of the War, even though it was in response to the horror of Belsen and Auschwitz after years of the Gestapo and SS.

Prisoners held in Scotland were not brutalised and broken. Food and fuel were scarce in Britain in the exhausted aftermath of the war. Life must have been bleak and harsh for the prisoners on Burrow Head, but they did receive enough clothing and nutrients to survive and there were a few lumps of coal for the stove. Most eventually returned to their families, unless the Communist Iron Curtain had slammed shut on them. Some remained to work on local farms and marry local girls, becoming over the years Galloway men with unusual accents.

At the edge of the caravan site there is an unpleasant rubbish dump of rusting cars, mouldering mattresses and similar detritus which have been thrown over the cliff.

It would be great if people from the continent could show us how to build holiday cabins in stone and wood to replace the metal ugliness of caravans, but it is doubtful

that the vines and quinces of Bavaria could thrive in the salt spray of winds that send spume flying over the cliff tops like a snow-fall.

The traditional pilgrimage to Whithorn included Ninian's grave at the Priory, the kirk at the Isle, and also the cave on the

isolated foreshore where Galloway's first
bishop is reputed to have retired for quiet
contemplation away from everyday business.
This cave is a two mile stroll away from
Burrow Head along cliff-top paths, through
close-cropped grass as fine as any golf course,
and over streams where lush cresses fill the
clear water. There are no modern dwellings
on this deserted shore, but mild-eyed seals
bob in the waves, providing intelligent,
wordless company until the path descends
to a wide beach of shingle.

At the northern end of the beach is the
cave. Recent roof-falls and mud-slides have
reduced its size. Roman Catholics gather
here every August during their celebrations
in memory of Ninian. Bishops with mitres,
vestments and croziers process along the
shingle to celebrate the Eucharist. The
priests of the diocese bring the sacred wafer
to the mouths of hundreds of the devout.
The seals are amazed by the singing.

The geological fissure of the cave is a
modest feature, but its atmosphere is
special. Whithorn burgh and the village at
the Isle are busy with the noise of engines.
The cave only echoes to the sound of wind
and wave. Little votive offerings of flowers,
driftwood crosses, or pebbles lovingly laid
in patterns on the floor, speak volumes
about the continuing life of the faith in
those who are like salt and yeast, preserving
and enlivening the rest of us.

Moses removed his sandals before the burning bush, and Abraham was awestruck and dropped the knife he was going to butcher Isaac with—when they realised they were in the presence of God. The true religion of the Hebrews began with that renunciation of the widespread practice of human sacrifice and the realisation that God is closer than breath or pulse.

Other peoples took longer to renounce human sacrifice. By moonlight, the Celtic Druids slew drugged victims in a fearful bid to appease implacable fates. Ninian taught them the message of Moses and Abraham and encouraged them with the Gospel of the conquest of evil by the empty grave of Jesus.

Ninian meditated on what he would preach when he withdrew to this lovely cave. His preaching was mighty and his words were remembered by the descendants of those who had heard them. Great carved stone crosses stood by the cave a thousand years ago. Voices were raised in the glorious singing of large congregations in this place on more than one day in the year.

The outline of simpler, cruder crosses were carved into the cave wall by pilgrims centuries ago. The carvings, of course, could not be moved to the Whithorn Museum when roof falls caused the remaining stand-ing crosses to be removed. Instead they remain on the walls as a reminder, amid less

mindful graffiti, of the long centuries of
the simple faith which still teaches sharing
not greed, gentleness not violence, peace of
mind not material wealth and a restless
soul.

The institutions of the Church have not
always been as gentle as the teachings of
their founders. The Celtic Church co-
existed with pagan rites for many centuries.
Conversion was a slow and gradual process.
Pagani (*payzan* = peasant = pagan) is the
Latin word for 'country people', for 'rustics'.
Initially the Christian religion in western
Europe was an urban phenomenon. Country
folk were more conservative by nature and
often cleaved to age-old customs when their
market town and the notable families of
the district became Christian.

It was the same in the Celtic world. But
in the Middle Ages, the Church horribly
persecuted the followers of 'Wicca' and the
'Way of Wyrd'—the thousands of so-called
witches and wizards burned at the stake
across Europe. Doubtless black magic and
great spiritual evil exists, but ecclesiastical
intolerance and doctrinal hostility towards
those who disagree is a terrible blight on
the Church. 'Heretics' were also tortured
to death in public displays of sadism.

In defence of the mentality of late
mediaeval Christendom, the Continent had
just emerged from the horror of bubonic
plague that virtually halved the human pop-

ulation. The link between fleas on diseased rats in insanitary cities was not understood as the source of the disease. It was thought to be the work of evil wizards and witches —hence the violence of the response.

The Protestant Churches were no more innocent than the Roman Catholic institutions. There were enough cruel Pharisees in Scottish Presbyteries, to the undying shame of the Kirk.

Throughout the centuries of its history, the Church has not been without sin. It is a wise pilgrim who looks to his or her own conscience before returning to the world from the cave. Faith needs some hesitancy, some doubt even, if it is to avoid arrogance and its resulting cruelty. It is difficult to abandon pride, to accept and recognise sin in oneself and find the release of humility. Humility is not the cringing and wringing of hands of a Dickensian Uriah Heep, or the Holy Wullie depicted by Robert Burns. Humility derives its ultimate meaning from the Latin word *humus*, meaning of the soil, fertile, and containing the seed of all kinds of wonderful possibilities.

At Ninian's cave, over the centuries, pilgrims pronounced the words *mea culpa*, 'I am to blame'—and their priests absolved them of their sins. Joyful shouting and the chanting of *gloria in excelsis Deo*, 'glory to God in the highest', accompanied the steps of travellers journeying from their destination having found the place of their own personal resurrection.

This everyday miracle of interior healing still happens. At Ninian's cave, men and women are released from the burden of regret from years past, and step as lightly into the future as John Bunyan's pilgrim once he had reached the Gate of Decision.

Ninian's great contemporary in the earliest congregations along the shores of the northern Celtic Sea was Patrick, over the narrow waters in Ulster. Ninian's own words did not survive the centuries, but many of Patrick's still ring out. Attributed to his pen is an ancient song which still speaks of the joy and peace of those who out-faced the druids and in open conversation persuaded many that life is cupped in the hands of a divinity so wonderful that even the most despised slave can be made to shine like the sun and rise up on wings like eagles. The words of 'Patrick's Breastplate' are words of encouragement against all that is evil:

I bind unto myself today
The strong name of the Trinity
By invocation of the same
The Three in One, the One in three.
Of whom all nature hath creation.

I bind this day to me forever
By power of faith, Christ's Incarnation;
His baptism in the Jordan River;

His death on cross for my salvation
His bursting from the spiced tomb;
His riding up the heavenly way,
His coming at the day of doom:
I bind unto myself to-day.

I bind unto myself to-day
The virtues of the star lit heaven,
The glorious sun's life-giving ray,
The whiteness of the moon at even
The flashing of the lightening free
The whirling winds tempestuous strides
The stable earth, the deep salt sea
Around the old eternal rocks.

I bind unto myself to-day
The power of God to hold and lead
His eye to watch, His might to stay,
His ear to hearken to my need
The wisdom of my God to teach
His hand to guide, his shield to ward,
The word of God to give me speech
His heavenly host to be my guard

CHRIST BE WITH ME, CHRIST WITHIN ME,
CHRIST BEHIND ME, CHRIST BEFORE ME,
CHRIST TO WIN ME,
CHRIST TO COMFORT AND RESTORE ME,
CHRIST BENEATH ME, CHRIST ABOVE ME,
CHRIST IN QUIET, CHRIST IN DANGER
CHRIST IN HEARTS OF ALL THAT LOVE ME,
CHRIST IN MOUTH
OF FRIEND AND STRANGER.

7

The CAVE
to KIRKINNER

THE native religious response of the people of Galloway sprang from the rowan, the briar, and reverence before the forces of nature in new moon skies torn by lightening. It was later infused by the wisdom and love of the stories of the Galilean carpenter.

Looking south from the interior of the cave, an outline of naked rock frames a view of waves with distant land interrupting the horizon of the Celtic Sea—the Isle of Man. It is named after Manannan, the Celtic deity of the sea, the equivalent of the Mediterranean Neptune.

Smaller lumps of solidity lie closer to the Machars—the Scar Rocks, or the skerries which used to be home to great colonies of seabirds. Their guano stained the skerries white—in sunshine they looked like small, snow covered peaks. These days, winter rain darkens them instead. The collapse of fish populations through commercial over-fishing deprived the birds of their food and famine came to the Scars. Only a fraction of previous numbers of birds still survive there, too few to whiten the rocks with their dung.

Great waves often pound the shingle of

the beach at Ninian's cave. This is a treacherous coast for boatmen. In the ninth century a ship of weary refugees from Northumbria embarked from the upper Solway in a desperate attempt to reach the Isle of Whithorn. But the weather was against them. Their boat was overwhelmed by great waves as they entered the harbour and part of their very precious deck cargo was washed overboard. Since the tides wash up much flotsam and jetsam on the beach at the cave, the refugees, who managed to reach the land, were delighted when their lost cargo was discovered on the tide line at Ninian's cave. It was declared a miracle.

The precious cargo in question was encased in a stout wooden travelling box which had floated to safety. Within the box was the marvellous copy of the Lindisfarne Gospels which still survives—a glorious example of the illuminated manuscripts that Celtic-inspired Christianity produced. In Mediaeval times, these Gospels were called 'the book which fell in the sea'.

The refugees were monks who had been driven by the Vikings from Lindisfarne, the little island from which the Celtic Church had begun its mission among the northern English. They carried with them their two most precious possessions, the Lindisfarne Gospels, and the revered remains of Bishop Cuthbert, after whom Kirkcudbright is named.

But the Northumbrian refugees did not
find lasting refuge in the Machars. The
horror of the Viking longships was to
descend on Galloway too. Thankfully the
wandering guardians of Cuthbert's coffin
and the Lindisfarne Gospels kept their
treasures safe until the Vikings were defeated. Then the saint's body was reburied at
Durham and the great cathedral built over
his bones.

At the far end of the cave's shingle, a
stream has carved a little valley through
the grassy cliff. Upon a rise above the
stream are the remains of Port Castle. The
stonework of walls which predated the
Vikings can still be seen, but the path away
from the coast follows the sound of the
stream through woodland in which snow-
drops, daffodils, bluebells and wild garlic
bloom in sequence. Pheasants, bred like
poultry, peck their way through the under-
growth and occasionally burst out from
under the feet as though the dire month of
October and the shooting season had already
arrived.

Many argue that the raising of game
birds for blood-sport is an activity which
has upset the ecological balance of the
countryside. Victorian gamekeepers used
poisoned bait, snares, traps and ruthless
guns to destroy populations of any kind of
predator which might take game birds
away from the sport of the landowners. As

a result there was an explosion in the population of voles, rabbits, mice and rats one summer in the Borders—over-keen gamekeepers had almost destroyed the owls, hawks, foxes, weasels and stoats which controlled the rodents.

In addition, huge areas of pastureland had been wasted by the voracious rodents. Cattle, horses and sheep went hungry, and sackloads of cats had to be imported from Edinburgh. Nowadays the poisoning, trapping and shooting is at an end—it is now outlawed, and the remnant populations of certain species are now protected by legislation—but the laying of snares for foxes still continues. These steel wires on ratchet loops inexorably tighten to bring a slow death. It is a pitiful sight to come upon a snare and find a bright fox strangled, or an old badger weak in a pool of blood. If foxes must be contained, then let the gun do it. At least it is swift.

The track beside the stream continues on until it reaches the large farmsteading of Kidsdale. Many holidaymakers with cars drive here before walking down to the cave. The fields around Kidsdale are fertile and protected against sea winds by great belts of mature, deciduous trees. The farmer has embarked on an enterprise only practised elsewhere in the Machars at the walled garden of Galloway House—raspberries and strawberries are available for sale in their seasons. A fine punnet of fresh fruit can be a delight after walking the miles from the Isle.

Some travellers will be content to travel only a mile or two further and rest for the night in Whithorn. Others will wish to walk a greater distance before nightfall.

At the time of writing, agreement for the official route of the Whithorn Pilgrim Way ends at Kidsdale. Many travellers will consider their journey complete, having visited the Priory, Isle and the foreshore at the cave. A bus service from Whithorn can swiftly return the traveller to the pace of the modern world. Others may wish to leave the peninsula more slowly. Although not yet signposted, quiet country roads and farmtracks wind north eastwards towards Newton Stewart. The first settlement of any size on the route is Kirkinner, eight miles from Kidsdale.

The road from the fruit field leads to-wards a cross roads with great overhanging beeches shading the tarmac. Cyclists who have followed the Pilgrim Way to the Isle will not be able to get their wheels around the footpaths from Burrow Head to Ninian's Cave, but they can follow the main road from the Isle towards Port William until they reach this crossroads and then turn onto the road to Kidsdale before the short walk to the shore. But, for those who have already visited the cave, the road to

Whithorn lies ahead, the road to Kirkinner
to the left.

The Isle to the Port road is wide and
traffic is fast, but the verge is broad. This
district is the parish of Glasserton, its name
a corruption of the Latin *ecclesia*. Glasserton,
or 'Churchtown', contains a lovely, old kirk
sheltering in trees. The congregations of
Glasserton and the Isle recently joined
forces with Whithorn in the shared effort
to find funds for a minister's stipend during
these years of public indifference to religion.
The old Free Kirk at the Isle has been
threatened with closure. Will it be converted into a garage or something similar? A
decision has been reached to concentrate
such funds as are available on the mainten-
ance of Glasserton Kirk.

Like many other rural parishes, whose
population has mostly departed for the
cities, this quiet building in the woods of
Glasserton has fallen into some disrepair.
Ivy grows through the vestry roof, but it
still carries the polish of someone's care
even though little money has been spent on
it for years past. The door is needfully lock-
ed against thieves, but by peering through
the windows the visitor can see one of the
most lovely kirk interiors in the Machars.

Below the pulpit is a long communion
table. It was the custom for the people to
gather round the table in their turn when
the rare and special Communion Sunday

was held. Rough bread and pewter goblets sufficed to administer the sacrament on spotless linen. On many Sundays this old kirk remains shuttered, no longer used for divine worship. People have got out of the habit. It is so much easier to switch on the television at home and enjoy some jolly hymn-singing on the screen. But is that really enough?

Beside the junction with the gravel road which leads to the kirk is a memorial to the men of Glasserton who were killed in the two World Wars. Sorley McLean, the great soldier poet of the Gaelic Hebrides, wrote 'we did not grudge the hardy soldiers of the enemy their courage'. As this long list, and others like it in every community throughout Scotland, declare, it was no easy matter to break and disarm the armies of Imperial and Nazi Germany. The list is horribly long. Young men who used to plough as straight as an arrow—their names are here.

Not far away is a small sawmill which scents the air with resin. The next few miles bring the smell of trees and earth. The tang of the sea falls behind with every step. The road for Kirkinner leaves the Port road and follows the signposts for Ravenstone. This quiet road intersects with the Pilgrim Way from the White Loch to Whithorn, before leading through farmland to the tangled woodland surrounding the ruins of Ravenstone Castle.

Many landowning families had grown rich in producing food for the burgeoning populations of the cities during the Industrial Revolution. This situation ended in 1846 when the Westminster government passed the Corn Laws allowing the import of cheap agricultural commodities from abroad. No longer was British agriculture protected by high tariff barriers against imported produce. Industrial pressure groups wished to lower production costs by minimising the wages given to their labour force. This they could only do if the high price of food was lowered.

The Corn Laws, however, were a victory for the industrial magnates and a defeat for the vested interests of the landowning aristocracy. Cheap foreign grain from Poland and the American prairies flooded into the market. Soon, refrigerated steamships were bringing in meat from Australia and New Zealand. The price paid to the Scottish farmer for his produce collapsed under the competition, and with it the ability of a tenant to pay an inflated rent to his landlord. The boom days for landed families was ended.

Conspicuous consumption dwindled into faded gentility. The ending of social status and financial muscle was gradual, but the economic crash of 1929-1931 bankrupted many ancient families and ruined more. Government taxation on large houses

coupled with socialist inspired 'death duties' became too great for diminished incomes. Roofs were removed from many grand, old houses to end the tax liability on them. This fate befell Ravenstone Castle, one-time site of a strong tower and later of a large Georgian mansion. Dense woodland hides the evidence of the changes which ended the dominance of this aristocratic residence over the surrounding countryside.

Not every landed family lost heavily in 1931 or as a result of socialist legislation. Huge areas of Scotland are still owned by landlords whose big houses are maintained by the rents of tenant farmers and whose lawyers and accountants have found means to avoid paying high levels of taxation. Half of Scotland is owned by five hundred estates!

The Danes, who manage to beat us in our own markets with everything from butter to bacon, used to suffer a similar problem. Their aristocratic 'junkers' dominated the Danish countryside as much as any Scottish laird, and, as Burns wrote, the tenant had to 'thole the factor's snash', *ie* to endure the cheek and arrogance of the land agent of the landowner, or endanger the continuation of their lease. The factors in the Highlands who cleared the indigenous human population for sheep-ranching have been justly reviled. Danish peasants likewise endured genera-tions of crushing poverty under rack-renting landlords.

Change only came to Denmark, Scotland's closest continental neighbour when a land tax was introduced. It was a graduated tax. Payments increased with larger areas of estate ground owned. The result in Denmark this century has been that the junkers sold their estates to tenants, and retained only small, family farms for themselves.

If the Ravenstone farmers had lived elsewhere in Scotland, they might still be tenants. As it is, local farming families bought their farms after World War II and they take as much pride in their own acres as the Danes.

Beyond the woods which surround the ruins of Ravenstone Castle is a vista of fields and plantations of conifers. Ranks of spruce now grow on ecologically sensitive wet-lands through which deep drains have been cut. One enterprising farmer in the locality mines his drained bog for sweet burning peat. Deep drainage ditches bar the way to cross country walking, but the roads in the interior of the peninsula are quiet and pleasant to walk.

This is drumlin country formed by huge clay mounds which were smeared across the landscape by Ice Age glaciers. Their slopes are well drained and fertile, making good pasture. The low ground between them used to be a pattern of lochs and marsh which in Ninian's time were dotted with inhabited crannogs. Dowalton Loch in the

centre of the peninsula was the largest and
once contained an archipelago of habitations.
Geese, ducks, wildfowl and fish once teemed among the reeds. They are gone, drained
away, but they can still be seen with the
mind's eye. They might return if an ecologically sensitive form of organic agriculture
were to replace the rush to capitalise on
subsidies from the common agricultural
policy of the European Community.
Because of this policy in recent years, across
western Europe wildlife habitats have been
destroyed while enormous mountains of
surplus food have rotted in a hungry world.

Just before the junction with the quiet
road from Sorbie to Whauphill, there is a
steep little valley with a rushing burn. This
used to be the outflow from the destroyed
Dowalton Loch, and the rush of its waters
were once constricted by the waterwheel of
Ravenstone Mill whose great stones ground
grain into flour.

Is it too unrealistic to suppose that in
wiser times a small weir in this valley could
restore Dowalton Loch? Conifers would
have to be felled and compensation paid
for flooded fields, but such a weir could
produce a useful amount of electricity if a
water-turned generator were to be installed.
The harvesting of wild eels and traditional,
non-intensive fish farming, combined with
the profit of electricity generation, would
create jobs as it did wherever watermills

used to turn in previous centuries. The Machars are certainly well situated for the garnering of renewable sources of energy. Wind farms are increasingly seen as cost-effective. It will not be long before their sails turn against the winds off Luce Bay.

Beyond Ravenstone Mill, the route to Kirkinner leaves the tarmac to follow a grass-grown farm track over the Bing Hill.

Salt water was last encountered at the cave on the west coast of the peninsula. The track now leads over the gentle swelling of Bing Hill between hedges until the Wigtown Bay coast north of Garlieston comes into view.

If a walker has rested the night in Whithorn after visiting the cave, quiet roads lead from that royal and ancient burgh to Garlieston. It is possible to follow the coast northwards. At first the coast beyond Garlieston is as wooded as Rigg Bay, where a good track leads between trees with a rocky shore tumbling to the shallow, sedimented waters of Wigtown Bay. Names like the Brandy Hole are evocative of furtive, moonlit journeys by smugglers, but on a summer day these woods are loud with the sound of bees feeding on pollen.

At Innerwell, the coastal track comes to a salmon fishing station where stake nets reach out onto the muddy expanse at the head of the bay. Thousands of salmon used to be caught here as the great fish gathered to run the gauntlet of anglers on the Blad-noch and Cree which were their ancestral spawning grounds. Only a remnant population still return from the ocean.

Beyond the smokehouse smell, the nature of the coastline is quite different from any other encountered in the Machars. The Kirkcudbright hills are now close across the waters, with a patchwork of fields and woods rising up to moorland, purple with heather in the summer. Innerwell, however, marks the beginning of flat, fertile estuarine farmland behind a tidal merse of salt marsh. Beyond this lie the immense sandbanks and mudflats over which the tide rushes. Quick-sand, glutinous mud, deep channels and a swiftly rising tide make the area dangerous for the unwary, though it is possible to follow a muddy path along the merse to the Bladnoch estuary.

Every winter, tens of thousands of geese overwinter at the expanse of Wigtown Bay. When their skeins first fly across the autumn sky, the cold wind of winter is not far behind. The wild goose was the symbol of the Holy Spirit for the Celtic Church. They did not consider the quarrelsome, cannibalistic pigeon a suitable candidate, but they admired the geese. Watching an arrowhead of geese parting the sky, calling to each other, it is worth observing the role of the leader. He has to labour harder than the others to create the slip-stream in

which those who follow more easily fly.
When the leader tires, his role is taken by a
fresher companion. Thus co-operative effort
enables companies of geese to travel further
and faster than an unaided individual could
manage. Geese are also faithful birds who
pair for life, mourn a dead partner, and care
diligently for their young. These noble
animals have been growing in number
recently, but a new threat now endangers
them.

The mud of Wigtown Bay contains vast
quantities of molluscs. A Dutch company,
specialising in producing pickled cockles
for the market, recently moved into the
area, their continental sources having run
out due to pollution and over-fishing. They
fitted powerful suction pumps onto fishing
boat hulls and, with this destructive
equipment, extracted vast quantities of the
molluscs, causing great harm to the
environment upon which geese and other
species depend. Legislation has halted this
process, but the damage has been done.

The human population of the planet has
doubled since World War II. As a result,
sea and land have been plundered for food.
As our species grows in numbers, every
other species of life diminishes in unequal
competition against us.

If the mud of the merse is not attractive
for walking, a small road from Innerwell
leads towards Kirkinner. Behind the salmon

fishery is a still pond, quite unlike the more rugged lochs and lochans elsewhere in the peninsula. It is named after a fifth century saint called Kennera. We will meet up with her at Kirkinner—'Kirk Kennera'—the little village whose gardens and apple trees nestle in fertile farmland a few miles away.

Indeed the village comes early into view from the high ground of the Bing Hill, where crows wheel and caw over green drumlin hills, where woods and plantations lie scattered throughout the fields. The hedges are full of life, with wrens flitting among shadows. Brambles, geans (wild cherry) and sloes droop with blossom and berries as the ancient, grass-grown track descends towards the village.

This centuries old roadway has not degenerated into an impassable barrier of thorn as so many others have for it is owned

ARIEL VIEW *of* KIRKINNER

by people who practise labour intensive, organic agriculture. Their farmyard is full of poultry pecking in the sunshine. Friendly, hand-reared Ayrshire cows graze between the hedges of the track. A traveller should repay the kindness of these pioneers by ensuring that all gates are closed behind them.

Kirkinner is situated on the main Whithorn to Newton Stewart road. Traffic, though not heavy by city standards, often travels at speeds which are careless of the lives of the children who live there. Modern bungalows and traditional stone cottages line the road. With an excellent shop and inn and several houses with bed and breakfast facilities, Kirkinner offers the first refreshment for those who have travelled across the interior of the peninsula from the cave.

At the south end of the village there is a tennis court and bowling green. Behind the manicured lawn of this courteous game is the stone tower of an old kirk surrounded by tall trees. The story of that kirkyard can wait for now.

Kirkinner Inn has a delightful garden in an orchard which is worth a visit. The Inn offers a well-earned rest after the long miles from the Isle.

8

KIRKINNER *to* NEWTON STEWART

KENNERA was a woman of the mid fifth century. In later times, women were not encouraged to play prominent roles in the Church, and the accusation is justly made that Christianity had by that time developed into a male-dominated organisation that excluded women to the seclusion of the nunnery.

The early Church knew things differently, however. In Bede's eighth century Northumbria, Hilda and Ebba were women of immense influence. In Ireland after Patrick, Brigid of Kildare, the daughter of a slave, was the most admired Christian in that island. All were active, powerful women. So was Kennera.

We do not know where she was born. Some traditions say that she was a native of Britain, others that she came from the German Rhineland. She certainly visited Britain, but it was beside the Rhine that she died.

The story associated with Kennera begins with a party of pilgrims returning from Jerusalem. In the summer of AD 450, their journey had taken them to the Rhineland. There they were slaughtered by the Huns

led by Attila, who had invaded the lands of
the German tribes.

Known as the *Hsiung Nu* to the Chinese,
the Huns, fierce nomads from the steppes
of Central Asia, had been thwarted in the
east by the building of the Great Wall of
China, a construction that dwarfed Hadrian's
Wall in Britain. They fought as mounted
archers, with the recent innovation of the
stirrup to steady them in the saddle. The
arrows and whips of this pitiless Asiatic
invasion of Europe brought the same
misery as the gunpowder and whips of
later European invasions of Aztec and Inca
civilisations in the Americas. Huns, and
other similar Asian tribal groupings, were
one of the principal causes of the collapse of
the Roman Empire, for Germans and Slavs
were driven before the Huns, weakening
the defences of the Empire until the Legions
were destroyed.

Among the party of British pilgrims
slaughtered in the Rhineland there was a
princess called Ursula. It was Kennera who
was appointed to travel to Britain to tell the
king of his daughter's death. Kennera may
have been one of Ursula's original travelling
companions, or she may have been a local
German girl. Whatever her background,
she must have been a tough individual to
risk travelling across a Europe at war with
itself. It is said that she did not remain in
Britain, but returned to Germany.

Kennera is remembered for organising famine relief and medical care in the wake of the warfare. After many active years she was murdered on the orders of the Queen of the Rhineland, who was jealous of her influence over the king. Kennera was undoubtedly a member of life's awkward squad. If she lived today, she might be seen wearing tweeds and sensible shoes, or twinset and pearls – or, should it be a ring through a nostril, leather and denim?

The only dedication of a parish in Britain to Kennera is at Kirkinner in the Machars of Galloway. It is impossible to verify the truth of the traditional story, but the association of Kennera with the Whithorn peninsula suggests that Ursula was of the royal house of Galloway, then part of the great kingdom of Rhyged which incorporated Cumbria across the Solway as well as Galloway. If Ursula was from Galloway, then the tradition that a royal princess had made a Christian pilgrimage to Jerusalem is eloquent in its recognition of the achievements of the earliest Church of Ninian.

The present parish kirk of Kirkinner is situated up a narrow lane behind the main street of the village. At the entry of the lane there is the village school with a fine monkey puzzle tree in its grounds. Opposite you will find the War memorial with a steel helmet set into stonework above a

The MONKEY PUZZLE TREE,
KIRK *and* WAR MEMORIAL, *at* KIRKINNER

long list of names. These men were once infants who played beneath the monkey puzzle tree.

In the village graveyard, set a field's length to the west of the village, are the names of other young men who met violent deaths. Twenty three of them from Scotland, Ireland, Wales, England, Czechoslovakia, South Africa, Canada and Australia lie buried. With them is the headstone of a young volunteer from Ohio who signed up to fight the Nazis before the United States entered the War. Every November a small crowd gathers, one villager at each headstone, to place a poppy in remembrance.

The dead men were members of aircrews who were training at RAF Baldoon for service against the U-Boats in the Atlantic. They crashed while training.

Baldoon airfield itself was built in the first year of the War, down on the flat land to the east of the village, where the River Bladnoch enters Wigtown Bay.

Kirkinner used to be a wilder place than it is now. It had a thousand young men on its doorstep. Local enthusiasts still fly light aircraft from the runways and the old hangars are used by commercial enterprises. The Nissen huts of conscripts, however, have all been cleared away. In dry weather the foundations of the township of huts are revealed by patches of parched grass.

More recently, when those who survived the War have grown old, unemployment has blighted a younger generation. The industrial, urban economy offers no hope of employment prospects brightening. Development of the rural economy could provide gainful, useful employment for millions.

When Robert Burns lived two hundred years ago, nine out of every ten Scots lived in small, rural communities. The Industrial Revolution and the clearances of the native population in the Highlands and Lowlands reversed that ratio in the century that followed. Many now argue that it is time to even out the imbalance. This could be done if ecologically benign methods of organic food production and forestry were developed. Many jobs could be created on the land and in processing produce for sale.

If this was coupled with determination to develop neglected sources of renewable energy, such as tidal barrages (the Solway has several potential sites), wind, wave and hydro power, then hundreds of thousands of jobs could quickly be developed in the ruralities. Rural society would be revitalised and urban tensions could be defused. Simple, new homes for the new settlers would be required and dwellings could be cheaply constructed on the old RAF foundations at Baldoon.

Facing the Nazis threat, ordinary people, both men and women, accepted conscription. Millions were equipped and sent thousands of miles to complete appallingly difficult tasks. Perhaps our modern city lifestyle and the abandonment of agriculture to chemicals and machinery endangers our future every bit as much as those more obvious enemies.

Past economic slumps like those of the 1930s were brought to an end by massive investment in armaments. If we are to win the struggle against environmental degradation, then investment must be made in the countryside. There are no more prairies and virgin forests in other continents for our urban unemployed to colonise, as they did last century in New Zealand, Australia and Canada. But the native soil of Scotland and its kindred countries beside the Celtic Sea could benefit from repopulation.

What other future does the conventional political or economic mind have to offer the unemployed poor? It is difficult to be patient after fifteen years of empty promises. Cardboard city and ever decreasing benefits from the post-War legacy of the Welfare State do little to encourage hope in the dispossessed.

Alternative visions of wiser and more equal social organisation still persist, and a visible symbol of that vision is the kirk in Kirkinner. It is beautifully proportioned, but like so many ecclesiastical buildings it is in some disrepair. Despite peeling paint-work, cracking plaster, sagging lead in the windows, eroded mortar in the stonework, loose slates and damp timbers, this fine old building is a treasure house.

It contains the thousand year old Kirkinner Cross which is in the care of the parish and still adorns a place of worship. It has escaped being sent to a sterile museum like so many others. Wonderfully intricate in its interlaced carving, it once stood out of doors to mark a preaching place of the Celtic Church. It stood in what later became the glebe grounds, the minister's acres behind the kirk.

This rolling field forms a natural amphitheatre. Children's voices still relish in finding the echo within it. Such natural acoustics would have been an aid to preaching, the reading of Scripture, the leading of prayer, and the delight of singing and music.

It is not fanciful to think of Ninian himself standing here beneath skeins of overflying geese. Kirkinner was a notable place even then, sheltering as it did beneath the protection of the nearby Ring Hill fortified camp which commanded the headwaters of Wigtown Bay.

Every parish in Scotland, from the Mull of Galloway to Yell and Unst in Shetland, has its glebe ground. These thousands of varied acres are free from the complicated tangle of property rights and vested interests, mortgages and deeds of trust which ensnare the use of private ground. These glebes could be developed as nature reserves and for pioneers of the new agriculture which is so badly needed by city and village alike.

There used to be a railway station in Kirkinner. It was possible to travel to Glasgow and return in civilised comfort in one day. Bungalows have been built on the bulldozed platform and the bridge which carried the single track has been demolished, but the embankment of the old railway still curves through the fields. Elsewhere in Scotland, disused railways have been converted into long distance walking and cycling routes that are free from motorised traffic. The cost of creating these public amenities is a fraction of the cost of constructing half a mile of high speed roadway. If the three miles from Kirkinner to Wigtown could be redeemed from a tangle of thorns, briars and nettles, then the journey northwards would be more pleasant.

In the meantime, the modern walker or cyclist has little option but to follow the main road. A whale-backed drumlin behind the old station yard divides Kirkinner from the neighbouring community of Braehead. Kirkinner was the kirk town, but Braehead grew up around the mill, where oatmeal was ground by a fast flowing stream to provide a staple in the diet of people who enjoyed the then plentiful salmon daily at certain times of the year.

Two miles to the north of Braehead the road swings in a great curve down to Bladnoch bridge. It spans the furthest reach of tidal salt water with its graceful arches.

If traffic on the main road and the lack of pavements make walking almost unbearable, it is possible to follow a slightly longer detour down onto the old Baldoon airfield.

It is also possible for the adventurous to avoid the Bladnoch bottleneck if Kirkinner is left off the itinerary. Quiet roads through Whauphill lead to Dalreagle Ford and stepping stones a few miles upriver. This is only negotiable in dry weather when the river is low, but travellers who use it are rewarded with the lovely, ancient stone circle of Torhousemuir on their route.

Beside Bladnoch bridge, on its southern shore, are some distinctive Victorian red brick buildings. This old creamery is now shuttered and silent. Hundreds of people used to work here in cheerful shifts among the steam. Pitiless economics recently made them redundant and local milk is hauled elsewhere for cheese-making.

Crossing the Bladnoch is not quite like crossing the Jordan, or the Rubicon, but in a sense this ribbon of water is the barrier which isolates Whithorn's peninsula from the mainland of Scotland.

At the far end of the bridge there is a small village and some industrial buildings which are more usually associated with the Highlands. Bladnoch Distillery used to produce the most southerly single malt whisky in Scotland. Bottled sunshine and

BLADNOCH BRIDGE *and* DISTILLERY

BLADNOCH DISTILLERY

malted barley to warm the innards came
from oak casks in great storage sheds in
which the young liquid was aged. Evapor-
ation through the casks diminished the
volume of liquid and the disparity between
what went into a sealed cask and what came
out after years of maturation was traditionally called by stillmen the 'angels' share'.
If the day was windless, the scent of the
'angels' share' used to waft past the bridge.

Sadly the distillery was closed in June
1993. The village of Bladnoch still offers a
good inn, but the distillery no longer
provides a free dram to visitors after guided
tours around its premises.

The county town of Wigtown is only a
mile away on its round, green hill. It was
from here that Kings of Scots tried to
establish Norman earls in the place of the

independent minded Celtic lords and princes of Galloway. Earls with the golden belt of the distant king's authority around their waists did not find the turbulent mixture of Celt, Northumbrian and Viking—the mediaeval Gallowegian—an easy subject to bend to royal authority. At Wigtown these earls built a castle and beside it a nunnery and priory to cater for pilgrims.

Like Whithorn, the main street of Wigtown still follows the pattern established by the foundations of mediaeval houses. The street swells out into a wide market area. Cattle, sheep and horses were brought here for sale. These animals are now taken by lorries to the market in Newton Stewart. Gardens and a bowling green have been created where anxious beasts used to steam and pant.

ARIEL VIEW *of* WIGTOWN

Wigtown played a terrible role during the 'Killing Times', when the dragoons of Charles II and James VII persecuted the Galloway Covenanters. Stubborn prisoners, who would not accept the claim of the kings in London to be the head of any Christian Church, were confined in the dungeons of the burgh Tollbooth. After being tortured to reveal the whereabouts of Covenanting companions, many were executed or shipped to the Caribbean where they were worked to death alongside African slaves in sugar plantations. The royal courts which dispensed this 'justice' were in Wigtown.

One of the most foul episodes of this shameful persecution involved the cruel deaths inflicted upon an old lady and a young girl. When the two Margarets refused to renounce their adherence to their Presbyterian convictions, they were taken to stakes dug into the sand of Wigtown Bay. As the tide rose they were slowly drowned before an appalled crowd. Repugnance at the viciousness of the king's officers destroyed the loyalty of the ordinary people of Galloway to the Stuarts of London.

Meanwhile, Highlanders bravely fought for the old royal house of Scotland in 1745 and died for their cause at Culloden the next year. Ordinary Gallowegians formed ranks in Hanoverian regiments to destroy them.

The political tradition of British Tories has its roots in the squires and lairds who supported the Stuart kings during the civil and religious unrest of the seventeenth century. Their great political opponents until the rise of nineteenth century liberalism and twentieth century socialism were the Whigs, who established their power base by opposing the supposed right of the monarchy to absolute and dictatorial powers. They advocated the constitutional tradition of the Crown having sovereignty only through Parliament. The name of this great political tradition echoes that of Wigtown, the place where the moral authority of the Stuarts reached its nadir.

Wigtownshire farmers drove their cattle with the cry *'whiggam! whiggam!'* When Galloway Covenanter regiments closed with their enemies, it was with the low growl of *'whiggam!'* in their throats. Their battle cry gave the name to the political tradition which established the foundation of parliamentary democracy. It is an achievement worth the memory.

The walker leaves Wigtown at its eastern end, beyond the grandiose County Buildings and the more modest parish kirk with its squint steeple. The County Buildings were built in an ornate style reminiscent of turn-of-the-century Paris. The District Court still meets here, but the administration of the local authority in Wigtownshire is now centred in Stranraer.

The Moss Road from Wigtown to

Newton Stewart has little traffic. It follows the low country beside the loops of the tidal River Cree. At the edge of town is a pathway leading over the salt merse to where the two Margarets were drowned. It is a place which chills the body, but can also warm the soul. God is never mocked with impunity by violence against the poor and weak. Evil always consumes itself and goodness endures.

Plantations of conifers accompany the Moss Road. Among the trees are the skeletal outlines of utilitarian brick buildings which were constructed in World War II. This was a great munitions factory which created thousands of tons of destruction.

The Cree winds close to the road and then loops away across the fields. Two hours of easy walking brings Newton Stewart in sight. Dramatic hills sweep around the town and the mountains of Galloway rise behind. Newton Stewart first came into being in the eighteenth century when textile mills were built to utilise the power of the flowing River Cree.

Today the town is by-passed by the A75 and is no longer choked with Irish lorries. A recent survey throughout Britain declared Newton Stewart to be the most polite community in the north of the island! It is a friendly, cheery place, more prosperous and lively than the older, quieter towns of the Machars.

Buses are available to take the adven-

CREE BRIDGE, NEWTON STEWART

turer from the Pilgrim Way to Glasgow,
Dumfries and London, but some may wish
to continue into the wild and exhilarating
mountains for the solitude in which to
digest the experiences of the journey before
returning to the world.

For those who need overnight rest,
Newton Stewart and its neighbour Minigaff
on the eastern bank of the Cree have everything from a hostel, bed and breakfast
establishments to a luxurious hotel with
sauna. Gastronomic varieties are available to
restore the weary after exertions in the fresh
air. For those who venture into the mountains these are the last delights of civilisation before the emptiness of the moors.

Newton Stewart and Minigaff are towns
to be enjoyed and their shops are full of the
necessities of living as well as the luxuries.

9

Over the HILLS *to* AWAY

MANY a traveller from the Whithorn Pilgrim Way will be reluctant to return to what passes for normality in our modern world. A short week of walking can cover the miles between Stranraer, Whithorn and Newton Stewart, but that might not be enough. If so, the Galloway mountains are for you.

Minigaff, on the eastern bank of the River Cree, is a much older settlement than Newton Stewart. One of the largest horse fairs in south western Scotland used to be held here.

Minigaff was situated on the Old Edinburgh Road. It was a military route constructed through Galloway so that reinforcements could be rushed to Ireland by the London government if rebellion or French invasion threatened. It was designed for the needs of marching regiments and its gradients and bends are unsuitable for modern motor traffic, therefore its surface was never smeared with tarmac. It is free of traffic and leads through the great sitka and larch plantations of the Galloway Forest Park until it meets up with the Southern Upland Way in the hills above

Clatheringshaws Loch. It also intersects with
the great Dover to Inverness cycle route.
The Whithorn pilgrim could continue an
unbroken journey to the east coast of
Lindisfarne, or even further onwards to
metropolitan Canterbury in the garden of
England.

A more rugged route into the mountains
follows the Penkiln Burn up a lonely valley,
before the path climbs the pass between
Curleywee and Millfare. These peaks are
dramatic, rising to over two thousand feet.
The path leads half way up the mountains.

If the day is clear, the climb to the top
is worth the effort. The view encompasses
the hills of the Hebrides and Ulster, and
then it is farewell to the gentle, green
Machars of Whithorn as the path descends
beyond the pass to the waters of Loch Dee.
This is harder and harsher country, often
trapped by snow in the winter.

In Autumn the cry of red deer stags is
heard beneath the wings of eagles. Wild
goats subsist in the sourest of country and
owls fly soundlessly through the night.

Robert the Bruce began his campaign
against the English occupation of Scotland
from these hills. His maternal blood flowed
from the ancient Celtic line that had survived unbroken since the time of Ninian.
His paternal blood came from the Norman
Lords of Annandale. The Galloway
mountains were the ancient hunting runs

CLATHERINGSHAWS LOCH

of his kin and in them he outfoxed an English force and destroyed it at Loch Trool. This flame in the south of Scotland ignited renewed resistance in the north, and the final and conclusive episode of the War of Independence had begun.

Centuries earlier, his ancestors had campaigned from these mountains to force the coastal settlements of the Vikings to accept their overlordship, and with it the re-emergence of Whithorn as a Christian centre.

At White Laggan, where the path from Curleywee descends to the forestry road beside Loch Dee, is a small and basic bothy. It is used by long distance walkers on the Southern Upland Road.

Kirrierioch, Merrick, Craigeasle, Cairngarroch, Monshalloch, Jarkness and Benyellary are a few of the names of the stark mountains which hem the horizon.

The bothy at White Laggan was once the simple home of a shepherd who, with his wife, raised their family by the light of paraffin lamps. During the middle of the week, and out of the holiday season, the bothy is usually quiet. At other times it is lively with conversation. The new Whithorn Pilgrim Way and the Dover to Inverness cycle route will increase the number of visitors at White Laggan. Thankfully it may be possible for many more simple bothies to be provided for those who travel quietly, away from motor traffic. Sitting by the fire in the bare interior of the cottage, with the wind driving against the plastic windows, you can let the mind wander.

Simple cabins, the use of two feet or two wheels, could open up the world to generations who think that horizons can only be broadened by motorways and aeroplanes.

Commercial tourism has often caused problems for host communities, from Nepal to Benidorm. The pilgrims of earlier centuries were not an equivalent threat to the well-being of the indigenous societies through which they passed. On the contrary, they brought variety to enrich the lives they encountered, and nationalism became *inter*nationalised. Nation spoke peace to nation through pilgrimage. The commercial world of giant scale tourism, on the other hand, can appear as a variation of beggar-my-neighbour.

Walking or cycling mean travel at a less arrogant pace. Few possessions can be taken. Status is not in what one owns, but in what a person becomes. Trade for food and lodging is basic and decent.

Scientists who monitor the chemical soup which is the atmosphere of this planet warn that our use of fossil fuel-powered transport is one of the critical factors which threaten us all with global warming, rising sea levels and an inadequate veil of ozone.

Walking and cycling and the use of public transport bring the world into range. The Galloway hills are a good place to sit and consider the urban motorway with its six lanes of traffic snarling along. Pollution from our cities is threatening to bring sterility to the lochs, rivers and moors. Acid rain leaches through thin soils, poisoning trees, and destroying organic water life. In some Galloway lochs, not even algae thrive. The lochs have become utterly barren.

The countryside needs people for it to bloom. If ever the cities attempt to recolonise the countryside in the struggle to avert ecological catastrophe, the motorway network of Britain could find a new use as linear villages of colonists with public transport along them. Then they would be good places to walk, fringed with gardens, ripe with fruit trees, with inns and shops along their miles, and with trams and buses when the legs get weary.

A wise man once said that 'we may need all our past to find our future'. The Pilgrim Way leads through the past in an attempt to discern a better future, and yet the doubt that covers this future is caused by the internal and unresolved conflict within humanity which causes war and every manner of suffering. The Christian Church brought a Gospel which gentled barbarian times, and yet at the end of the second millennium the surviving institutions of the historical Church, both Protestant and Roman Catholic, are largely disregarded by the public. The vast majority of people are interested in the deeper mysteries of life, and three quarters of Scots declare belief in God. Yet less than one in twenty still attend Christian worship in increasingly ageing congregations.

The Church has everything it needs to lead into the future. Its parishes have the potential to gather people into more self-reliant, co-operative communities, restoring initiative to the locality. The Gospel points away from mere material acquisitiveness and love and generosity make every good thing possible in the future. Thus we can say the words of John Bunyan:

Who would true valour see
Let him come hither;
One here will constant be
Come wind or weather;
There's no discouragement
Shall make him once relent
His first avowed intent
    To be a pilgrim.

Who so beset him round
With dismal stories
Do but themselves confound;
His strength the more is.
No lion can him fright,
He'll with a giant fight,
But he will have a right
    To be a pilgrim.

Hobgoblin nor foul fiend
Can daunt his spirit;
He knows he at the end
Shall life inherit.
Then fancies fly away;

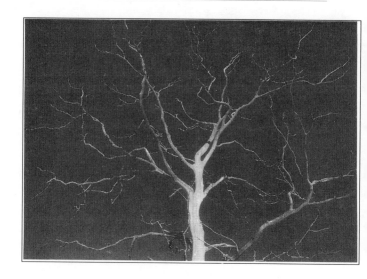

He'll fear not what men say;
He'll labour night and day
  To be a pilgrim.

The question to return home with is—
Will the days of my living harm the planet
more than they heal it? Pilgrimage is taking
the decision to become part of the cure, and
finding practical ways of doing so.

Some people might consider the text of
this book to be back to front. They may
consider the better direction to be from
Newton Stewart to the Isle, ending at
Glenluce Abbey.

Either way, the choice is yours.